THE WEALTH OF STATES:

POLICIES FOR A DYNAMIC ECONOMY

by
Roger J. Vaughan
Robert Pollard
and
Barbara Dyer

Norma Prasad deFreitas
Production Manager

CSPA
Hall of the States
400 North Capitol, Rm 291
Washington D.C., 20001

On the cover: Diego Rivera, The Making of a Fresco, San Francisco Art Institute.
Photograph by Don Beatty © 1984

Library of Congress Cataloging in Publication Data

Vaughan, Roger J.
   The wealth of states.

   Bibliography: p.
   Includes index.
   1. Economic development.   2. Economic policy.   3. Entrepreneur.   I. Pollard,
Robert, 1945–   . II. Dyer, Barbara, 1951–   . III. Title.
HD87.V38   1985   338.9   85–29082
ISBN 0-934842-23-X

Manufactured in the United States of America

CSPA is a membership organization comprised of the planning and policy advisers to
the nation's governors. Located in Washington, D.C., the Council provides assistance
to the states on a wide spectrum of policy matters. The Council carries out policy
research on both state and national issues. The Council was formed in 1966 and has
been affiliated with the National Governors' Association since 1975.

This technical assistance study was accomplished under a grant with the
Economic Development Administration. The statements, findings, conclusions,
recommendations, and other data in this report are solely those of the authors and
do not necessarily reflect the views of the Economic Development Administration,
CSPA or its members.

CSPA
Hall of the States
400 North Capitol Street, Suite 291
Washington, D.C. 20001
(202) 624-5386

James M. Souby
Executive Director

TABLE OF CONTENTS

FOREWORD

For decades state development agencies have acted on the belief that the wealth of a state depends on tax abatements and low interest loans given away to attract out of state businesses. States have offered low or no taxes, low-interest loans, subsidized land, and even free membership in the local country club, and less influential taxpayers have been left to foot the bill.

While pursuing the economic development fad, states have neglected the basic business of government—educating their population, maintaining their infrastructure and creating a stable fiscal environment. These are the most powerful economic forces under state control.

New plants and major relocations, which receive such notoriety—like the siting of GM's Saturn Plant—are responsible for less than 5 percent of the new jobs in most states. Actually, more than half of a state's new jobs are created by new enterprises, not just new branches, and almost all by residents of the state. Forty percent are from the expansion of the state's existing firms, mostly small ones. Growth comes from within, not without. Individuals willing to take risks, to innovate, operating on their own or within existing businesses, are the engine of growth in all states.

This book makes the point that evolving state economic policy should place more emphasis on establishing a sound fiscal environment, regulation that encourages competition rather than protection, quality in education, and long-term planning of public works. This will create an environment for entrepreneurship that will expand and diversify the state economy from within. During an era of rapid change, this is the best insurance state's residents can have.

IMPROVING THE ENVIRONMENT FOR ENTREPRENEURSHIP

States can improve the climate for innovation through several means. First, they can reform or abolish certain regulations. For example, state restrictions on entry to professions and industries are often barriers to new business formation. Though originally designed to protect consumers, they have rapidly become a way of limiting competition.

Second, states must create a competitive financial industry. New enterprises need capital, but they also tend to be risky investments. State and federal regulations may discourage risk taking by lenders. Usury ceilings, regulations governing new issues, and restrictions on the portfolios of state chartered banks, public pension funds, and other financial institutions should all be reviewed as part of any serious long-term state development effort.

Third, states should stabilize their fiscal environment. Lowering tax rates or offering abatements to attract business usually requires raising taxes later to compensate for revenue shortfalls. A tax structure that provides sufficient revenues over a period of time to finance state and local investments in education and public works, coupled with a stabilization fund that accumulates revenue during good times to supplement revenues during bad times, are the basis of long-term fiscal stability.

INVESTING IN PEOPLE

The quality of a state's education system—from primary school to graduate school—is its most important development program. The rapid pace of technological advance and its unpredictable twists and turns threaten every skill and occupation with obsolescence. Economic development depends on how quickly and how well people can acquire new skills. Three steps are vital:

First, states can extend student loans and grants to encompass more training, education activities, and people. This would provide both low income people and gifted students with a wider range of opportunities. But, this step should be taken only by those states that have established a sound loan program with low defaults and a high collection rate of defaulted loans.

Second, states should only support education and training institutions if they are performing well. The mystique of the education process has allowed educators to escape the discipline of evaluation. Money should only go to those schools that are measurably educating or training their students and placing them successfully in jobs.

Finally, states should encourage the provision of such information on the performance of its schools, training institutes, and universities to all those contemplating an education program. At the very least, states should publish placement rates and surveys of initial earnings of graduates of all post secondary programs from all institutions (public and private) in the state.

PROVIDING THE INFRASTRUCTURE

Infrastructure—transportation networks, water supply and treatment systems, and other public facilities—are necessary for economic development. Economic downtrends of the 1970s forced delays in appropriate maintenance expenditures. Such spending has only recently increased—reversing a long-term decline.

But, increased spending alone is not enough. A major obstacle to identifying needed infrastructure projects is a lack of information on the current condition of existing facilities and the demands that are likely to be made of them in the future. Some states have begun to remedy this situation by conducting surveys of their public facilities.

Others are improving capital planning through developing more systematic means for determining future public works needs, for evaluating projects, and for forecasting the impact of public works on future operating budgets.

CONCLUSIONS

The primary message of this book is that state development policy must change to reflect the changing nature of the economy. The policy of pursuing firms may have been appropriate when the dominant economic trend was economic deconcentration, with large manufacturing corporations moving out of the nation's industrial belt.

Today the pattern is different. For large corporations to remain competitive, they need a well-educated labor force and an adaptable local education and training system. For entrepreneurs to create a growing share of new jobs and innovations, states must remove the barriers posed by obsolete regulatory policies and uncompetitive financial institutions. Sustained development will require the commitment of planning and management as well as money to public works investments.

State economies will continue to be dominated by national and international forces, but by deploying the resources they do control more effectively, states can create a much more favorable environment for development than was possible by targeted tax abatements and indiscriminate loan subsidies.

Governor John H. Sununu, New Hampshire

ACKNOWLEDGMENTS

This project was funded by the Economic Development Administration. Many people contributed to this book and must share in any credit. They are, however, exempt from responsibility for points that are factually wrong or disagreeable.

John Sununu, Governor of New Hampshire, served as lead governor and chairman of the advisory board. Without his efforts this project would never have begun. Dutch Leonard, Associate Professor, the Kennedy School of Government provided invaluable advice and suggestions at all stages in the production. Professor Karl Case chairman of the Economics Department at Wellesley College carefully reviewed the final as well as an earlier draft. An advisory board met in December 1984 and March 1985 and generously gave their time and many thoughtful comments and criticisms. The following served on these groups: Richard Baznik, Case Western Reserve; Robert Benko, Pennsylvania Office of Policy Development; R. Scott Fosler, Committee on Economic Development; Robert Friedman, president, Corporation for Enterprise Development; Richard Geltman, National Governors' Association; Dick Hage and Brandan Roberts, Economic Development Administration; Richard Harrington, President, National Association of State Development Agencies; Mike Hickey, director of economic development, New Hampshire; William Kynock, Florida Office of Planning and Budgeting; Helen Ladd, Kennedy School of Government; Ira Magaziner, president, Telesis Inc.; Robert Miller, AmeriTrust Corporation; Richard McGahey, New York University; Shelley Metzenbaum, Kennedy School of Government; Hugh O'Neill, deputy secretary to the governor of New York; Pete Plastrik, executive director, Governor's Council on Jobs and Economic Development, Michigan; Michael Piore, professor of Economics, MIT; Doug Ross, director, Michigan Department of Commerce; Mary Jo Waits, Arizona Office of Planning and Policy; and Cicero Wilson, American Enterprise Institute.

Others have reviewed drafts at different stages and offered advice and assistance: Tom Berkshire, Assistant for Policy Analysis to the governor of Illinois; Steve Hull, Communications director to the governor of Florida; George Humphreys, Department of Economic and Community Affairs, Oklahoma; Leonard Wheat, Economic Development Administration; June Sekera, Massachussetts Department of Labor; and Jacques Bagur, Gulf South Research Institute, Louisiana.

PROLOGUE

When the price of cotton was high, Mississippians had no use for industry. They even passed a law to keep new industry out. Cotton reigned for decades, and, except for a brief spurt from the lumber business around the turn of the century and the occasional tannery or charcoal kiln, Mississippi was a "one company town."

By the 1920s the economy had begun to change. Soil erosion was "killing the cotton fields," foreign competition had driven cotton prices down, new machinery had taken the place of many farm-hands, and unemployment had grown. The state's leaders realized that cotton alone could no longer provide a decent standard of living for Mississippians. The state needed to diversify its economy.

Mississippi's commitment to economic expansion occurred at a time when innovation was transforming the national economy. The development of high-speed and low-cost transportation, the extension of power transmission systems and natural gas lines, and the availability of inexpensive air conditioning allowed industry to expand into new areas. Mississippi capitalized on this opportunity. By opening up natural gas fields and developing transmission systems, it offered electricity rates that were competitive with any in the country.

Yet two major obstacles to industrialization remained. The state had a wealth of natural resources but little capital and business expertise. To remedy these gaps, the legislature enacted the Balance Agriculture With Industry Program (BAWI) in 1936. The program was the State's "declaration of independence" from cotton. It offered financial incentives to attract industrial enterprises from outside the state's borders. BAWI authorized municipalities to issue bonds to prepare sites and build plants for private firms and exempted certain classes of industry from *ad valorem* taxes for five years.

For a while BAWI was considered an unequivocal success. Mississippi communities offered land, factory buildings, and five years of "life without taxes" in exchange for investment and jobs. Signs along major rail routes, glossy advertisements in magazines and a multitude of news stories sang the praises of the "new industrial frontier." By the end of World War II—10 years after the program's inception—firms producing glass, textiles, automobile tires, meat products, and ships employed more than 180,000 Mississippians.

BAWI was the central economic development strategy in Mississippi for decades. But all was not rosy.[1] Most of the new plants were low-skill, low-wage operations that had fled the pressures of northern labor unions. Local tax rolls were shortchanged by agreements, sanctioned by state law, to waive all local property taxes for 10 years. Local property taxes were used to finance the entire cost of industrial buildings. Some unscrupulous operators moved into the state only long enough to enjoy the tax-free benefits.

The most comprehensive financial incentive program of its time, BAWI proved to be a mixed blessing. It accelerated the pace of business diversification, but it also trapped Mississippi into a tradition of low-wage industries and denied tax coffers the resources for basic investments in education, infrastructure, and public health at levels enjoyed elsewhere. And, despite its leadership in establishing the prototype for state economic development strategy, Mississippi remains one of the poorest states in the nation.

This is not the end of the story for Mississippi. The state has moved beyond relying on industrial recruitment as its sole economic development tool, is attempting to improve the quality of elementary and secondary education, and is promoting basic research. Governor William Winter expressed this broader view of development policy:

> A trained and educated citizenry—that's our ultimate defense. We can build all the battleships anybody can sell to the Defense Department and spend all kinds of money for military hardware, but if we don't have an educated citizenry, then I don't think we've accomplished anything.[2]

Traditionally, education policy has not been thought of as part of an economic development strategy. States have only begun to wrestle with how to make the investments in knowledge and ideas required in a modern economy. They are confronting the economic implications of neglecting investments in public infrastructure. And they are attempting to adapt their regulatory policies to rapidly changing technologies.

Economic development has become a broad issue. But how should state resources be deployed? What state activities influence economic development? What strategies will work politically? Elected leaders continue to promise their constituents jobs and development. How can those promises be translated into an effective economic strategy? These are the topics of the following chapters.

CHAPTER 1

INTRODUCTION

Elected officials are expected to promote economic development. Plant closings, rising unemployment, or failures to attract new businesses to the state create vocal and dissatisfied groups, each with its own agenda for economic action. In the nearly 50 years since Mississippi invented the industrial recruitment strategy, governors and legislators have responded to these demands with programs designed to attract or retain industry.

Yet many of these programs have not proven successful. The number of relocating plants is shrinking, and firms in the emerging service sector are not as susceptible to traditional inducements. A broader approach to development is needed to match the changing economic environment. This book offers that new approach.

First, the goal of economic development is to create wealth. Wealth is our capacity to produce those goods and services that we value, and includes not only those items whose value is established in the market place but also nonmarket goods and services such as a clean environment, justice, and public safety. While job creation is the result of successful policy, it is not in and of itself the goal of economic development. Some state programs that have sought to create jobs in the name of development have actually impeded economic development. For example, by subsidizing a firm to move into a state, taxes paid by other firms are driven up, impairing their competitive position.

Second, we expand our capacity to produce when risk-taking individuals and public agencies discover and develop better ways to use resources.[3] Public sector activities play a vital role in establishing the climate for entrepreneurial activity by establishing and enforcing rules and regulations and by making needed investments in education and infrastructure.

Third, many traditional development policies—such as industrial recruiting and public works programs—have limited capacity either to spur development or to create jobs.[4] On the other hand, many government activities not traditionally regarded as development strategies—such as investments in education and infrastructure and regulatory reform—have a much greater if unexploited potential.

Finally, development policy is conducted in perennial conflict. As purchasers of goods and services, we all benefit from greater choice and lower costs resulting from innovations. But as employees, resource owners, and stockholders we may lose in the development process. To the worker who loses a job because of new labor saving technology or an increase in imports from abroad, the availability of new products will seem poor compensation. To the investor whose investment fails because the company could not compete, progress brings little reward. The displaced worker and the disappointed investor are part of a constituency that may oppose development. A successful development strategy must include not only the right policies but also ways of resolving or reducing the economic and political conflicts inherent in the policy making process.

One reason why policy makers focus on job creation is that the wealth creating process is not easily visible and is poorly understood. A plant closing receives more attention than the thousands of innovations that spawn new enterprises and new divisions within existing firms. These innovations often create many more jobs than were lost in the shutdown. The second reason is political. The pressure on elected officials to do something immediately leads to policies that have (or appear to have) quick and readily observable results, sometimes without regard for their long-term consequences. Politicians also favor measures that provide benefits directly to their jurisdictions; wealth creation provides much more diffuse benefits.

Spurring the pace of development requires a broad based strategy that spans many state activities. Achieving this end requires the chief executive not only to design legislative and administrative initiatives but also to build the political support needed to carry them out. Each chapter lists some of the policies that might be considered for inclusion in a state's economic development strategy.

Because some of the concepts used in this book have attained lives of their own with many special meanings, we should also stress three conclusions *not* reached in the book.

First, although the development model described in the first three chapters focuses on the entrepreneur as the driving force behind development, this does not exclude the majority of the population from the development process. Entrepreneurship refers to all individuals willing to take risks to test their innovation in the market place. This includes all types of people from all regions and neighborhoods. Far from excluding those with few resources and little business training, those with low incomes seem as able to succeed in innovative enterprises as anyone else. Entrepreneurship is not limited to venture capitalists or to those with advanced engineering degrees.

Second, the state economic development strategy described in this book is not aimed at "getting government out of the way". While some development programs should be cut back, others should be expanded. We conclude that many traditional economic development policies represent a misallocation of resources, but others should be retained as a signal to the business community of the government's continued commitment to development. Regulations should not be abandoned but, if possible, reformed to achieve their basic objectives without damaging the entrepreneurial environment. For education and infrastructure investments, the state must develop ways of getting a higher return on its investments and may have to increase its spending.

Third, the emphasis on programs to encourage development does not imply that equity considerations are not important. Governments at all levels have an important responsibility to create opportunities for those with low incomes and few skills. Many of the policies discussed in the following chapters would both create wealth and benefit the economically disadvantaged. There is not necessarily a trade-off between equity and growth in the development framework we suggest.

OUTLINE

This book is divided into three parts: 1) the theory of development (Chapters 2, 3, and 4); 2) how effectively three types of investment—business capital, human capital, and public infrastructure—are carried out (Chapters 5, 6, and 7 respectively); and 3) the political economy of development (Chapter 8).

Part 1: The Theory

Chapter 2 defines economic development as the process through which wealth is created. In a world characterized by imperfect information and change, there are opportunities in all communities to create wealth by using resources more effectively. In the absence of barriers, individuals will pursue those opportunities; the greater the rewards, the more energetic the pursuit. Public agencies can also create wealth and are particularly effective in areas where the benefits and costs of a good or service are not easily valued in the marketplace.

Chapter 3 shows how focusing on jobs has led us to misunderstand the underlying process of economic development. Some assumptions about how jobs are created that have guided economic development policies are based upon an incomplete view of the development process. The chapter also describes the weaknesses of industrial recruitment programs that have formed the core of most state job and economic development strategies.

A successful development strategy must create an environment that is conducive to entrepreneurial activity. Chapter 4 defines the most important element in this environment as competition, which will occur in the absence of restrictions to pursuing economic opportunities. As a result of policies to protect consumers from poor quality goods and services and to preserve local jobs, states have inadvertently erected barriers to entrepreneurship and competition. These include restrictions to entry in industries and trades, price regulations, and discriminatory tax policies. Economic development policy must take seriously the concerns that prompt some of these measures without constructing further impediments to development. This means carrying out policies that meet the stated public objectives without giving in to approaches promoted by vested interests. The entrepreneurial environment must also include the resources and institutions needed for investment. Although entrepreneurship is often associated with new and small enterprises, large corporations can also behave entrepreneurially if they operate in a competitive environment and reward initiative among their employees.

Part 2:   Investment

Entrepreneurial initiative is translated into development through investment. Chapters 5, 6, and 7 examine three different types of investment—business capital, human capital, and public infrastructure—and the public sector role in each. Chapter 5 explores the process of business investment. Public sector involvement in business investment is primarily (but not solely) in establishing the ground rules under which private investment is carried out. Taxes and regulations adopted to protect consumers or the environment inadvertently distort the flow of capital through financial institutions. These barriers to the efficient operation of capital markets are also barriers to entrepreneurship. Opportunities exist for states to improve the environment for entrepreneurial activity. These improvements can often expand economic opportunities for low-income people without sacrificing the original intent of the legislation or regulation.

Chapter 6 analyzes human capital investment—the ways in which people acquire education and training. The public sector must not only "set the rules" but also finance the education and training for those who cannot afford to make the investments themselves. Increasing the education and skill levels of the workforce may prove the most important element in a state's development strategy. The operation of labor markets is influenced by tax and regulatory policies and by the presence of state and local governments in education and training. A state's economic strategy should include initiatives to improve the efficiency with which people can invest in themselves.

Chapter 7 explores the state's role in infrastructure investment. Public agencies are concerned not only with financing public works but also with identifying and selecting investments. Planning, budgeting, and financing practices of state governments strongly influence how effectively state and local governments meet demands for public facilities. Efficient planning methods can strengthen the "market test" for projects and will thus weaken the importance of political considerations.

Part 3: The Political Economy

The last chapter lays out some economic and political guidelines for the design and implementation of a political strategy to build support for entrepreneurial economic policies. Governors must retain the support of their current constituencies, develop new constituencies to support entrepreneurial policies, and educate the public through a vigorous communications program.

THE CONTEXT

State economic policy should be understood in the context of the national economy and federal policy. The role of state government in economic development is limited. State economies are dominated by events in the national and international economies and by the actions of millions of individuals. State policies cannot by themselves produce economic prosperity, and, in the short run, most state policies will have only minor effect.

Although limited, the state's role is significant. Unenlightened state policies can be serious obstacles to development. Their taxing, regulatory, and spending powers help shape the long-term environment for development. States that have enjoyed the best economic health in recent years are those that have experienced bursts of entrepreneurial activity. Sustained economic development has proven elusive in those states that do not provide basic services such as the infrastructure to support economic development, an education and training system that imparts knowledge and skills efficiently, and an environment congenial to entrepreneurial initiatives.

Finally, state policies are undertaken for several different reasons. Economic development is important but it is not the only or even the overriding goal in many areas. Short-term political objectives, social equity, and quality of life for example, also factor heavily into the equation. Sometimes a policy that is sound from an economic perspective may make poor political sense. This book emphasizes the "economics" of public policies and makes no attempt to judge what makes sense from other perspectives.

The key to an effective economic development strategy is for the state to identify those functions that it can plan, manage, and coordinate efficiently and then execute them well. If the state expands its activities into those areas where it does not have a comparative advantage—however well-intentioned the policy—it is unlikely to achieve these new objectives and will be less effective in carrying out its basic duties.

NOTES

1. Peirce and Hagstrom, 1983.
2. Botkin, Dimancescu, and Stata, 1984, p.155.
3. Much of our annual output of goods and services does not depend upon innovation and entrepreneurial initiative, but upon the repetitive execution of tasks. However, to expand our ability to produce goods and services—to create additional wealth—requires entrepreneurship.
4. This book is not concerned with economic policies aimed at short term stabilization. A full discussion of state stabilization policies is given in Vaughan, 1980.

PART 1: THE THEORY

CHAPTER 2

CREATING WEALTH

The 52 year old multi-mixer salesman was astounded that one of his drive-in restaurant customers required 8 machines capable of producing 48 shakes simultaneously. He had to see the operation in person, even though it meant traveling to California from his home in the Chicago suburbs. His biographers described the experience: 'All through the day he watched crowds of customers waiting in line, more people than he had ever seen at a drive-in. At dusk the golden arches lit up the sky. The lines never seemed to dwindle. Ray Kroc was overcome and cried out softly to himself that this would go any place in the world.'[1]

The McDonald brothers were reluctant entrepreneurs. Despite numerous opportunities, they had sold only six franchises, and turned down a deal involving chain expansion. Kroc used all his skills to get them to agree to an arrangement that would provide them with 1.4 percent of the gross sales of the franchise. A few years later, the brothers offered to sell Kroc everything—the trademarks, copyrights, formulas, and name for $2.7 million. Kroc accepted.

☆ ☆ ☆

Betty Nesmith was employed as an executive secretary in a Texas bank and performed freelance artwork to make a little extra money. Tired of retyping work because of a minor error, she put some tempera waterbase paint in a bottle and used it to paint over mistakes. For six years she limited her efforts to mixing "Liquid Paper" for friends. She failed to interest IBM in marketing the product.

After experimenting in her kitchen to improve its quality, she finally decided to market Liquid Paper herself. She started the business with little cash and operated out of her own home—working part time as a secretary to support herself. Thriving as a cottage industry, the enterprise emerged as the Liquid Paper Corporation in 1968. When in 1978 it was acquired by the Gillette Corporation, Liquid Paper had worldwide sales of $38 million and more than 600 employees.

☆ ☆ ☆

Arthur Fry was stuck in a sticky situation. While singing in the North Presbyterian Church choir, he kept missing cues because bookmarks in his hymnal would fall out. What he needed, he reckoned, was a marker that would adhere to the spot yet not damage the page when removed. Then one Sunday, while daydreaming during a sermon, Fry, 53, a chemical engineer specializing in new product development for the 3M Corporation in St. Paul Minnesota, had a flash of inspiration. He remembered a product a colleague had discovered during an unsuccessful experiment—instead of a superstrength adhesive, he'd come up with a low-tack glue. Racing back to the lab, Fry found the substance not quite perfect for his purposes, it peeled off easily but still left a residue on the page—but his quest was launched.

Nine months later, Fry had perfected Post-it Notes those little yellow memo pads with a sticky edge on each page—the pages press in place and then peel off for reuse. 'You have to kiss a lot of frogs to find a prince,' explains Fry of his success.[2]

☆　☆　☆

Bennett Cohen, a pottery crafts instructor, and Jerry Greenfield, a biochemistry lab technician, had a long-standing agreement to go into business together. Their idea was to pick some specialty food that did well in big cities and introduce it into a rural college town. Bagel-making equipment was too expensive so they decided on ice cream. Saratoga Springs, New York, already had a premium ice-cream parlor so they settled on Burlington, Vermont.

Applying the knowledge they acquired from a five dollar mail order course in ice-cream making from Pennsylvania State University, they opened Ben and Jerry's Ice Cream in an old gas station in 1978. They later moved into larger quarters in an old spool and bobbin factory and began shipping pint containers to grocery stores. The company went public in 1984, and by the end of 1985 is expected to open a new plant capable of producing three-million gallons of ice cream a year. The company will have franchised shops over the entire East Coast. The business that started with a $12,000 investment in equipment and materials is now worth more than $5 million.[3]

☆　☆　☆

Donald Burr, an executive with Texas International Airlines recognized that deregulation of airlines in 1978 would create opportunities for new air carriers. In 1981, with three used jets, Burr's PEOPLExpress inaugurated service between Newark, New Jersey, and Buffalo, New York, Columbus, Ohio, and Norfolk, Virginia. Three years later PEOPLExpress had more flights into the New York area than any other airline and had transformed the under-utilized Newark airport into the fastest growing airport in the country.

Before deregulation, the Civil Aeronautics Board had prevented airlines from competing by offering lower prices. Burr gambled that there was a large, untapped market for no-frills, low-price air service. PEOPLExpress charges extra for baggage and offers no complementary beverages or food, but its fares in some markets undercut existing fares by as much as 75 percent. The stunning success of PEOPLExpress has forced many established carriers to lower their prices to meet the challenge and has offered many people the opportunity to fly who could not previously afford it.[4]

☆　☆　☆

Although trained as a chemical engineer, Adam Osborne's interests were in computers and his talents in writing. One of his books, **"An Introduction To Microcomputers,"** sold more than 300,000 copies. In the late 1970s, Osborne recognized a "truck-sized hole" in the computer industry. In 1980, using the profits from his consulting and publishing company together with funds provided by a venture capitalist, he founded the Osborne Computer Corporation.

The Osborne 1, the first portable microcomputer, weighed 24 pounds, cost $1,800, and came with enough software "to run a small country." Within two months of the first shipment, the company was profitable. By 1982 the company had sales of $80 million and was shipping 10,000 computers a month. In September of 1983, the company filed for reorganization under Chapter 11 of the Federal Bankruptcy Code. Osborne Computers could not compete with the superior products offered by its many emulators.[5]

☆　☆　☆

Kitt Taft had once worked in mechanical drafting, but when job prospects disappeared she took classes in massage. Still without work and living on welfare, she was pleased to hear that a new hotel in the neighborhood was planning a fitness center featuring massage services.

However, the hotel did not want to employ a masseuse; it wanted a self-employed contractor. Kitt could not afford to purchase the necessary table and oils and did not know how to bid for the position. She turned for help to the Women's Economic Development Corporation (WEDCo), a private, not-for-profit organization providing business assistance to low-income women. Together they put together a proposal, which the hotel accepted, and negotiated a personal line of credit from a local bank. Today she works as an independent contractor, has hired an assistant, and gives lectures.[6]

These people—salesman, secretary, scientist, pottery crafts instructor, lab technician, corporate executive, and welfare recipient—are all entrepreneurs. They risked their time and usually their own money betting they could produce new goods and services that consumers wanted (Liquid Paper, 3M, and Osborne), make existing ones available at lower costs (McDonalds and PEOPLExpress), or penetrate new markets with existing goods and services (Ben, Jerry, and Kitt). Each discovered a more valuable way of using resources and a new opportunity for consumers. They all expanded our capacity to produce and thereby created wealth. This is the core of economic development.

Fast food, liquid paper, cheap air travel, sticky note pads, computers, ice cream, massages, a new road, or a public school—these new opportunities increase our wealth.[7] This chapter examines how wealth is created:

> Wealth is our capacity to produce goods and services that we value. Economic development is the process of innovation through which we increase the capacity of individuals and organizations to create wealth. The goods and services we value include not only those items that are traded in marketplaces but also less tangible things—the quality of the environment, public security, and other elements that contribute to our sense of well-being.[8]

Development usually entails more than the growth of jobs, output, or income. It also encompasses the constant adaptations that we must make in the face of a changing economic environment. These adaptations include changes in lifestyle as more women join the labor force, changes in the workplace in response to new technologies, and changes in political alignments as economic opportunities are redistributed. The "recycling" of shrinking New England mill towns as computer firms replace textile mills is as much part of the development process as the rapid occupation of a new industrial park in the suburbs of a growth center in the South.

What changes count as additions to wealth will depend upon the perspective from which the changes are viewed. The relocation of a factory from the frostbelt to the sunbelt will not count as additional wealth from the national point of view—it is simply a zero sum game. But, from the points of view of both the losing and winning communities there has been a very real change. The emphasis in this book is upon those policies that are not zero sum games. However, these policies do not require development officials to act in the nation's interest rather than in their own interest. The policies are those that create wealth for residents of the state or local area and the nation.

The first section of this chapter outlines the overall process of economic development, focusing on the direct and indirect consequences of continuous pursuit of opportunities. The second section analyzes in more detail the importance of profits and losses in the continual learning process of economic development. The final section describes how public agencies can create wealth and the relative strengths and weaknesses of the public and private sectors in promoting development.

THE ECONOMIC DEVELOPMENT PROCESS

At the core of the economic development process is a deceptively simple mechanism with five components:

1. Opportunities

In any nation, state, or community, no matter how poor, there are entrepreneurial opportunities—chances for producing new goods and services, making present ones cheaper, or penetrating new markets.

For desperately poor communities such as Chicago's South Side, Los Angeles' Watts, or New York's South Bronx, it may seem impractical to discuss entrepreneurial opportunity. But many opportunities can be pursued almost anywhere—Betty Nesmith's liquid paper, Adam Osborne's computer and even Ben and Jerry's ice cream could be manufactured in any neighborhood within trucking distance of final markets. There are many other opportunities that could take advantage of the unique attributes of neighborhoods— their proximity to downtown, and low cost manufacturing sites for example. For example, in 1981 Gary Waldron set up a business to take advantage of the South Bronx's most visible symptoms of distress—the vacant land and unemployed people. He hired local participants in a job training program, rented vacant lots, and set up greenhouses to grow expensive flowers and cooking herbs for New York City's restaurants. Today he employs 51 people and operates the nation's most sophisticated hydroponic greenhouses.

Opportunities arise and new ones are continually being created because our economic environment is constantly changing and because our knowledge of how best to make and market products consumers value is imperfect and also changing. Changes in tastes, technologies, science, world trade patterns, and resource scarcities continually create opportunities for innovations in the way we use our resources to meet consumers' demands.

The model of development described here differs fundamentally from the simple economic models that have formed the basis of traditional models of growth: it accepts that information cannot be acquired costlessly. Entrepreneurs exist because no one has complete information, and therefore it is always possible to innovate. In the "free information" world of traditional theory, there would be no place for entrepreneurs because everyone would be putting resources to their most valued use automatically and would automatically adjust when changing resource prices or new technologies necessitated it. Entrepreneurs attempt to assemble better information and ideas than anybody else, then test whether they have done so in the marketplace.

Competition among entrepreneurs is first and foremost a discovery mechanism, and successful discoveries propel development. By contrast, traditional economics views competition in the marketplace as an allocative mechanism, which, under very restrictive conditions, allocates goods and services in an optimal manner. There is no "optimality" in the model described in this chapter—only more or less efficient mechanisms for discovering what goods to produce and how best to produce and distribute them.

2. Entrepreneurs[9]

The populations of all nations, states, and communities contain entrepreneurs—people willing to risk the time and effort to pursue opportunities if the potential rewards are large enough. The greater the incentives, the larger the number of people who will act as entrepreneurs, and the more intense will be their pursuit. For many goods and services, competition is the best way to find out how much consumers value alternative goods and services, the best way of producing those goods and services, and the best way of finding out who best meet consumers' demands.

A small community or state can experience spurts of growth of employment and wealth without entrepreneurial activity occurring within that region: a national housing boom causes lumber mills in Oregon to hire additional labor, which enriches the community; an automaker builds an assembly plant in a small community to replace an aging one elsewhere; a poor harvest in the Soviet Union creates a boom in the wheatbelt.

But sustained economic development implies the expansion of wealth—an increase in per capita wealth. Replacement investments may create economic development locally, but they do less to create development statewide or nationwide. To contribute to economic development, entrepreneurs must be innovative. They must discover a new product or service, develop a new way of making something, or find new markets to sell it in.[10]

3. Investment

The innovations of entrepreneurs become wealth through investment—the acquisition of the equipment, facilities, inventories, prototypes, and skills needed to produce and market the new goods and services. For many, the largest investment is their own time as they strive to develop and market their product. Entrepreneurs risk financial loss if their venture fails.

Entrepreneurs can rarely afford to pay for investments from their own resources and so turn to potential investors to finance their projects. The pace of economic development depends not only on the ability of entrepreneurs to innovate and their willingness to take risks but also on the efficiency with which the capital market accommodates their demands for financing (Chapters 5, 6, and 7).

4. Public Sector

Development will not occur simply as a result of the energies and imagination of entrepreneurs. Rules must be established and enforced for transactions among individuals, to protect people and property, and to achieve different social objectives. How well these rules and regulations are framed are important influences on the development process.

The public sector is also involved in making investments needed to sustain development. Entrepreneurs have little incentive to produce some of the goods that people value because they are collective consumption goods (public safety and basic knowledge, for example) that can be consumed without being paid for. Neither will private enterprise limit the amount of those goods and services whose production and consumption creates external effects such as air pollution, noise, or dangers to health. To ensure the efficient pursuit of these opportunities, government (or nonprofit) initiative is required.

15

Individuals and government agencies each pursue opportunities in different ways, but both translate their wealth-creating goals into investments in business capital, human capital, and public infrastructure—assets that increase our capacity to produce and hence our wealth.

5. Conflict

Economic development redistributes as well as creates wealth. The community in which a new enterprise is based will experience large benefits, while other communities in which the enterprise's competitors are located may be less enthusiastic.

For those few (but very important) innovations that displace established industries, the resistance from losers may be stronger than the support from those benefitting. The benefits in terms of new goods and services are widespread, the costs, in terms of lost jobs and devalued investments, are usually more concentrated. Therefore, a basic conflict exists between the pursuit of economic development and the political concern of preserving jobs and creating employment opportunities (Chapter 3).

Development policy must try and balance the conflicting demands of those displaced by development with the broader goals of expanding overall economic opportunities. It must manage the continuous process of economic replacement and renewal.

THE ENTREPRENEUR

Entrepreneurs create wealth incrementally. Ben and Jerry's contribution to development in Burlington, Vermont, cannot be measured by the value of sales or even gross profits because part of this gain is offset by the loss of output and profits among the competing ice cream makers and sellers they have displaced. The net increase in income in the community is a useful approximation but does not include the "consumer surplus" enjoyed by those buying the products. We do know that the community's wealth has increased as a result of the innovation because people have voluntarily selected Ben and Jerry's product over the others. Even new products such as automobiles, airplanes and computers displace or replace other goods or services.

If a subsidy paid for by local taxpayers is involved with the setting up of a new enterprise, we can be less sure that it represents a net addition to the community's wealth. (If the subsidy is paid for by a higher level of government, then the project creates wealth from the local community's perspective). In this instance, offsetting costs are not simply the lost output in displaced firms but the cost of the subsidy as well. A printing firm that expands in part because it receives low-cost land in an industrial park may not increase wealth if the cost of the subsidy added to the value of the business taken away from other local printing firms exceeds the value of the new firm.[11]

Politicians are concerned with who gets the wealth as well as with how much is created. Examining the employment impacts of development is a good way of gaining an impression of its distributional consequences. In fact, none of us takes the broad view of the changes that are created by development: as individuals, we are concerned about how development affects our lives; as elected officials, we are interested in how a change affects those in our district or those with whose interests we have become allied.

Even if the overall value of an innovation to consumers exceeds the costs to those displaced, the consumers may be spread nationwide, while those losing jobs may be concentrated in one state or community—as is the case with rising imports of automobiles, steel, and shoes.[12] If, from the perspective of a particular jurisdiction, the costs of development exceed the benefits, there will be political pressure to resist change and to preserve jobs.

Profits and Losses

The entrepreneurs described at the beginning of this chapter are unrepresentative—six out of seven succeeded. The vast majority of entrepreneurial ventures do not result in successful innovations and large profits. Ambrose Bierce defined an opportunity as "a favorable occasion for grasping disappointment." Discovering and delivering a new product or service that consumers regard as a better value than other things they are currently buying, or developing and installing a more efficient technology, or capturing a new market are formidable tasks when so many others have the same goals in mind. Entrepreneurs will only challenge these odds if there are few barriers to entering the industry (Chapter 4) and if the rewards for success are sufficient.

The rewards for success and the penalties for failure serve three vital functions as: 1) incentives; 2) signals; and 3) control.

Incentives. Risk taking requires rewards. People differ in their willingness to take risks. Entrepreneurship allows cautious people to avoid risk-taking while those who prefer a larger element of risk in their investments have the opportunity. When government under-takes investments, everyone bears the risks. For example, when the U.S. Synfuels Corporation abandoned its attempt to produce oil from shale, every American taxpayer shared part of the loss. In con-trast, when Osborne computer failed, the firm and its shareholders bore most of the loss.[13]

If someone can earn a tax-free and virtually risk-free return of 10 percent on investment-grade municipal bonds, why should he or she invest in a business enterprise with risky future earnings? Why should one invest time and effort in developing a new product with only a small chance of success? Part of the answer is profits. The chance to turn $1,300 (the proceeds from the sale of a used Volks-wagon bus and calculator) into assets worth more than $200 million (as Steve Jobs did with Apple Computer) is a powerful inducement to hard work and risk-taking. These rewards are important not only to entrepreneurs but also to those who provide them with the capital to get the venture off the ground.

Entrepreneurs may also be motivated by the desire for fame, power, independence, or other nonpecuniary goals. But money is an important motivator and is more directly influenced by public policy than are other motives. Overall, the greater the expected rewards in a venture, the more people will be drawn to the field, and the harder they will strive for success.

The magnitude of the rewards may seem completely out of pro-portion to the risks involved or to the value of the product. Whether it is right that the inventor of the pet rock became a millionaire as a result of nine months work or that oil companies made billions of dollars when OPEC increased the price of oil is an ethical or political issue about which economics is silent. Profits have been a popular target of politicians. Several European countries and American states tax "unearned" income more heavily than earned income, and Congress has enacted a windfall profits tax on oil companies. But because rewards are important to entrepreneurs and since it is not always possible to distinguish between the profits entrepreneurs earn because they are very skillful and the profits speculators receive because they are lucky, attempts to tax away the latter will dampen entrepreneurial enthusiasm.

Signals. Many successful entrepreneurs are emulators. They are not the first with a new product or process but know a good idea when they see one. Ray Kroc did not invent the fast-food restaurant, but he was among the first to recognize its potential. Long lines outside the McDonald brothers' stand told Kroc that big profits were being made inside. These profits indicated that consumers wanted more resources devoted to fast-food restaurants. Kroc and many others followed. Osborne was an innovator in personal computers and led hundreds of firms into the market—from established companies like IBM and AT & T to dozens of new firms.

Paradoxically, by attracting competitors profits are soon eliminated. The large but temporary profits earned by a successful innovator will provide the resources to finance research and development to continue the innovative process. The knowledge that other firms will soon be competing for those profits is a strong incentive to keep innovating.[14]

Control. The ability of people to pursue opportunities is subject to market tests; to fund a project entrepreneurs must be able to persuade lenders or investors that their proposed project has a reasonable chance of success (Chapter 5). Profits and losses indicate the would-be borrower's track record at discovering things that people value and at producing them competitively. Profits are a feedback mechanism for deciding who shall have command over resources in the future, or at what cost resources will be made available.

Some people believe that opportunity-seeking is a "zero-sum" game: if entrepreneurs make a great deal of money, it must be at the expense of their customers.[15] The opposite is true. If entrepreneurs are to sell their products or services to customers who purchase voluntarily, all parties must expect to benefit. As economist George Stigler has observed (1984, p.47):

> Henry Ford made a lot of money making cars at one time, but that was a small advantage compared to the millions of people who were, for the first time in their lives, emancipated from common carriers and could live where they wanted, move at the hours they wanted to places they wanted.

But some people suffered from Ford's innovation. Saddle-makers, blacksmiths, and carriagemakers learned new trades or went broke. Some would gladly have outlawed horseless carriages in order to preserve their wealth and jobs. But outlawing the horseless carriage would have cost society much more than the costs suffered by those who lost their jobs because of the motorcar.

In a lesser way, some people suffered as a result of the success of each of the entrepreneurs described at the beginning of this chapter. The purchase of an Osborne computer probably meant one less sale for Apple or another competitor. Each planeload of PEOPLExpress passengers meant fewer flyers on Eastern and other established carriers. However, the value of the new goods and services exceeded their cost to competing firms. (Customers preferred their Osborne computer at its low price to alternatives; passengers preferred their low-price PEOPLExpress flight to a more expensive flight on another carrier).

Many states have used business loan programs as a way of helping out companies in financial difficulty. They are usually drawn into the project to save local jobs. However, their intervention may not be successful in the long-run. Propping up a company that is unable to compete delays other entrepreneurs from filling the market gap. For example, propping up a printing firm or a bakery will take away business from other local printers and bakeries. It will also continue to use labor and other resources in a relatively unproductive use, which in the long run will handicap other local firms who could make better use of the resources.

Competition

Why are dozens of firms developing personal computers when most of them, like Osborne, must eventually fail? Why are many firms producing gourmet ice cream? Competition among entrepreneurs may seem wasteful, but in most instances it is the most efficient way of finding out which goods and services best satisfy consumer demands.

There is no way to predict in advance exactly what consumers want. If there were, some enterprise would have made a great deal of money marketing the technique to other companies. Despite extensive testing and market research, food-processing companies strike out with 80 percent of the products they introduce.[16] The failure rate for first novels is close to 99 percent. So many ventures end in failure because finding out exactly what goods and services people are prepared to pay for or what production methods will prove technically and economically feasible requires answering thousands of technical, managerial, and marketing questions. Many different permutations and combinations must be explored. Competition among entrepreneurs allows these to be answered more quickly than if one centralized agency were trying out alternatives. In proportion to the expected rewards, competition allows the most motivated and able people to tackle the problems of meeting consumers demands. And it limits those who must pay for the search process to those who are consciously taking risks.

The Osborne computer did not die in vain. Its temporary success alerted other firms (including IBM) to the importance of quality control, a large screen, and the dangers of announcing new products months in advance of deliveries. Failed food products make their parent companies a little more aware of what consumers want. Some of the entrepreneurs involved in failed businesses also learn the skills needed to run a successful enterprise. More than half of those starting up highly successful new businesses have failed at least once before.

The Limits to Entrepreneurship

While in many instances competition among entrepreneurs is the most efficient way of finding out what consumers want, it does not always work. Entrepreneurs do not always move resources into more valued uses. For example, if the production or consumption of goods creates external effects—costs or benefits for people who are not party to the exchange—then those pursuing profits may commit resources to a less valued use or fail to move them to a more valued one. Air pollution is a classic example of an external effect. Only a tiny part of the cost of air pollution is paid by an individual driving a car or operating a factory. The rest is borne by those living or working downwind of the polluter. Therefore, drivers and factory managers will rarely consider it worthwhile to install pollution control devices, even though this would be a valuable investment if the full costs of pollution were considered. Third party effects mean that the information and incentives generated in the marketplace are systematically misleading.[17]

As mentioned earlier, another instance in which private transactions will not allocate resources to their best use is when the goods or services can be collectively consumed. Because people can consume collective goods whether or not they pay for them, it is difficult or impossible for private businesses to collect sufficient revenues to pay for their production and maintenance. Therefore, public intervention is needed to ensure their production.

Finally, entrepreneurs look only at the economic consequences of their actions and do not consider the distributional consequences. There are limits to what employers can do for employees in firms driven out of business by competition.[18] Entrepreneurs are not concerned if the new product that they are bringing to the market causes firms to move out of inner city locations. They judge potential employees by their expected productivity, not by how much they may need a job.

Distributional consequences—both among groups of people and among geographic areas—are important socially and politically. A large part of federal and state budgets is spent addressing perceived inequitable distributional outcomes of the development process—providing assistance for the poor, the elderly, or those displaced by development. Elected officials are also concerned with how the benefits of development are distributed among geographical areas (Chapters 3 and 4). When an action involves resource reallocation on a large scale, the political process will tend to be drawn into the decisionmaking process. In these instances, the interests of the entrepreneur will often conflict with the those of elected officials.

WEALTH CREATION BY THE PUBLIC SECTOR

Managing the process of economic development is only one of the many mandates imposed on federal, state, and local governments. Public policies influence the economy in many ways, both deliberately and inadvertently. When private businesses cannot allocate resources efficiently or when the distributional consequences of private decisionmaking create inequities, the government has traditionally stepped in. The challenge to public decisionmakers is to decide when to intervene and to select the method of intervention that achieves public objectives most effectively. To do this, they must be aware of how public activities affect private wealth-creating activities directly and indirectly.

Producing and distributing goods and services efficiently is more difficult for public agencies than for private entrepreneurs. First, public agencies are attempting to achieve a more complex set of objectives than are private entrepreneurs. While the goals of a private enterprise may be expressed in terms of long-term profits, public sector objectives include justice, security, and fairness, areas that do not lend themselves to easy quantification and comparison.

Second, public agencies must consider the distributional consequences of their actions. The governor, who appoints agency administrators, and the members of the legislature, who oversee agency operations and approve budgets, all must answer to constituencies. They must be concerned with how the costs and benefits of programs are distributed among geographic areas, industries, and socioeconomic groups. A rigorous calculation of net present value with no analysis of who is affected will rarely win political approval for a project.

The importance of interest groups in the decisionmaking process does not imply cronyism or corruption on the part of elected and appointed officials. Because the objectives of public policy cannot be easily quantified, public administrators must determine how strongly people feel about an issue by sounding out groups that represent different public interests. Businessmen and women can rely on sales figures to measure people's wishes. The methods employed by public agencies must be much more subtle and less precise.

Third, the pressure to perform well is not as intense on public agencies as it is on private entrepreneurs.[19] Agencies are usually sole suppliers of goods and services and cannot learn from competitors. Public employees do not earn financial rewards that are tied to how successfully they have met consumers' demands or controlled costs, at least in the short run.[20]

Fourth, agencies usually have less reliable information on which to base their decisions than do private entrepreneurs. For example:

- Market prices, which provide entrepreneurs with valuable information about the prospective benefits and costs of a decision, are often unavailable or unreliable because the services cannot be priced in the marketplace or are provided at subsidized rates.
- Public agencies are denied firsthand knowledge of opportunities available to entrepreneurs, who are more likely to be aware of underutilized resources, innovations, and shifts in consumer tastes.

Finally, stringent "good government" rules that have been introduced to make it more difficult to misuse public funds or to ensure that equal opportunity goals are pursued can make it difficult to respond quickly and flexibly to the changing economic environment.

Nevertheless, the public sector has an advantage in many types of resource allocation decisions. These are activities for which the demand is better expressed through the political system than through the market system, including income redistribution, environmental protection, and public safety.

In addition, there are many nonprofit institutions that span the public and private sectors. These range from foundations that sponsor research concerned with social issues and community development corporations to health-care facilities and tollbridge authorities. They are too diverse to be easily characterized and have played a major part in the redevelopment of urban centers. Although their role in development will not be discussed explicitly in this book, they are likely to play a continuing role whenever development calls for a partnership between public and private sectors.

IMPLICATIONS FOR STATE DEVELOPMENT POLICY

Economic development is a process of innovation—discovering more productive uses of resources—and of creating more of the things that people value. Searching for more productive ways to use our resources and investing in the necessary capital—business, human and public infrastructure—is undertaken by both entrepreneurs and public agencies.

The public role in the development process extends far beyond those few programs targeted at development objectives to include much of the taxing, expenditure, regulatory, and enforcement activities of government. Government actions affect the relative cost of factors of production, the risks and rewards of opportunity seeking, the production and availability of information, and the quality of vital economic support systems such as water and transportation. Much of a state's influence is inadvertent. A state development strategy must be built on this broad view of the state's role.

The state strategy must also recognize the importance of the entrepreneur as innovator and investor. Many state development efforts have focused upon reducing the cost of business capital in communities by providing low-cost land and buildings and low-interest loans, incentives that have more effect on large, well-established corporations than on entrepreneurial activity.

NOTES

1. Boas and Chain, 1976, p.11. This description of the rise of MacDonald's is adapted from this book.

2. This description is quoted from **People Weekly,** December, 10, 1984, p. 105.

3. See Minsky, 1985.

4. See Carley, 1984.

5. See Rogers and Larsen, 1984, pp. 133-34.

6. Information provided by WEDCo, St. Paul, Minnesota. WEDCo is funded by grants from private foundations and from fees it charges clients.

7. The value of these new opportunities will not be accurately reflected in national income or product statistics. These data only record how much consumers paid for them, not how much they valued them.

8. It might be argued that people can feel better off without actually being better off. An alcoholic may feel better off when having another drink that is actually harming him. But the definition of what is better off does not come from some measurable, objective standard but from the individuals themselves—individuals are the arbiters of the value of the goods and services they consume. However, this "subjectivism" poses problems for economists. An excellent discussion of the issue of subjectivism in economics is contained in Rhoads, 1985, Chapter 9.

9. Jean Baptiste Say, the eighteenth century French economist who coined the term "entrepreneur," defined it as someone who moves resources from lower- into higher-valued uses.

10. Even in the most unlikely environments, entrepreneurs emerge to help find new and more productive ways of using resources. In Chinese agricultural communes,

recent economic reforms have created a tenfold increase in productivity (**Economist,** February 5, 1985). In prisoner-of-war camps during World War II, entrepreneurs emerged to create a lively market in food and cigarettes (Radford, 1946). An untapped group of potential entrepreneurs exists in all low-income neighborhoods as the experience of the programs discussed in the last section of Chapter 6 demonstrates.

11. Some people argue that most growth is not based on innovation but upon the simple expansion of productive capacity by extending the size of a plant and the number of machines. But if this additional output is to be sold, then new markets must be exploited or competitors beaten. Development requires innovation. Investments in plant and equipment made simply to replace worn-out equipment do not involve innovation, but then neither do they lead to development.

   A great deal of what is labeled economic development is nothing more than the redistribution of economic activity among areas—encouraging firms to relocate into distressed areas from elsewhere within a state or as a result of competition among states. Although the winners experience development, it is equal to the losses in other places—an outcome that may still justify the program, depending on the importance attached to redistribution.

12. Costs may exceed benefits if producing or consuming the product creates unpleasant side effects, such as air pollution, that do not enter into the calculations of producers or consumers. Some economists have argued that benefits may be less than costs because consumers do not pay for the unemployment in communities that had been dependent on making a commodity rendered obsolete by a new technology or by foreign competition (Kuttner, 1984). However, this argument ignores the fact that with every spending decision, jobs are created producing those things we buy and destroyed in those industries whose products and services we do not purchase. One cannot point to one type of consumer decision—for example, buying a Japanese car—and argue that it has higher indirect costs than other consumer decisions.

13. Because most business losses are at least, in part, tax deductible, taxpayers bear part of the cost of unsuccessful business innovations.

14. Some people have advocated that government should preserve the monopoly position enjoyed by successful innovators so that even more research can be undertaken (Magaziner and Reich, 1984). However, the same action that would increase a firm's resources would reduce the incentive. Morris and Mueller describe the process (1980, p.34):

   > monopoly rents [the rewards of being first] are short-lived. Each innovation is soon imitated, and then replaced by yet another innovation. The monopoly a successful innovator obtains gives him but a brief respite from the 'perennial gale of creative destruction' taking place in the free enterprise economy: monopoly rents give him the only means to pursue new innovations. Any firm that merely attempted to maintain and enjoy a present monopoly position would be doomed to extinction under the force of dynamic competition . . .

15. Steve Wozniak, one of the founders of Apple Computer, contrasts this view with one taught in an economics course at the University of California at Berkeley that he recently enrolled in: "I was going under an assumed name, Rocky Clark, so they didn't know who I was . . . My economics course was interesting. We had a socialist T.A. [teaching assistant] who taught that companies made money by cheating the consumer. All the kids in the class thought that companies would make a lot of

profit if they could figure out a way to cut the cost of a product down to make it cheap and rip off the consumer. I contrast that with the way we did things at Apple. Every product design decision was based on what consumers wanted, what would compete the best, what they would buy. We tried to do what customers wanted in our best judgment and give them high-quality products. So I would stand up in class and argue about what the T.A. was saying. After a while he started telling me to shut up or that he would kick me out if I interrupted him again." (**Byte Magazine,** January 1985, reprinted in the **Wall Street Journal,** March 18, 1985).

16. **Wall Street Journal,** February 26, 1980.

17. There are two ways of "internalizing" external effects. The most common is for the government to compel private parties to take costs into consideration—by regulating permissible levels of pollution emissions, for example. An alternative is to redefine property rights to include, for example, freedom from pollution, and then to allow for negotiation and litigation between polluters and those affected by pollution to internalize effects.

18. Some very successful entrepreneurs have used their profits to establish foundations dedicated to examining these issues, but these issues cannot be addressed in the regular course of business.

19. Many private firms also escape from the pressure to perform well. Firms protected by barriers to competition (Chapter 4) and firms that have achieved a monopoly position by other means will not suffer sharply reduced sales and profits if they fail to improve their products and services to take advantage of the latest ideas. By contrast, entrepreneurs in highly competitive industries, such as computers, fast food, or air transportation, experience immediate repercussions from making erroneous decisions or from not keeping up with their competitors.

20. In the long run, public employees will be held accountable by local taxpayers. If the quantity of public services continues to exceed that demanded by taxpayers and if the quality of services falls short, taxpayers will hold down local taxes (by voting for candidates committed to cutting taxes or by a tax-limiting referendum), which will necessitate public employee lay-offs.

CHAPTER 3

TRADITIONAL VIEWS ON ECONOMIC DEVELOPMENT

Although economic development has been a top priority for many governors, direct expenditures on economic development—including the budgets of state departments of commerce and those of various public development authorities—average about 2 percent of state expenditures.[1] Indirect expenditures on development-related activities—including education and training programs and public works projects—are much larger.

In the absence of a theory of development to indicate which policies would be most effective, states have relied upon rules-of-thumb to help design development programs. Their concern has been to find ways of exerting the greatest possible impact from the expenditure of modest state development budgets. State efforts have concentrated on finding ways of targeting their programs toward areas that appear to have the greatest potential for development. This chapter examines some of the most widely held assumptions that have been used to shape development policy:

- The purpose of economic development policy is to create jobs;
- Development programs should be targeted on growth industries, which are: 1) export industries; 2) high value-added industries; 3) small businesses; and, most recently, 4) high-tech firms;
- Programs should focus on recruiting large firms from out of state and on retaining large firms in state.

Each of these guidelines contains an important kernel of truth, but as an organizing principle for a state development strategy each will cause states to overlook development opportunities and even to adopt inappropriate policies. These issues are addressed in turn in this chapter. The first section looks at the way we analyze what is happening in the economy and concludes that we may be misled if we rely on traditional indicators of economic performance alone.

DIAGNOSING THE ECONOMY

During the 1970s, the apparently sluggish national economy was buffeted by a tenfold increase in energy prices, double-digit inflation, interest rates that topped 20 percent, and an unprecedented increase in foreign competition. Labor-force participation by women grew from 39.3 percent in 1965 to 51.3 percent in 1980. And technological change shifted the composition of employment toward information processing and away from material processing. The fact that the economy was able to accomodate these changes and create jobs rapidly is scarcely a symptom of stagnation.

Facts do not speak for themselves. An economy undergoing rapid development may transmit many of the same statistical signals— high unemployment rates, low capacity utilization, and declining output in basic industries—as one that is languishing. Both emit symptoms of decay—plant closings, lengthening unemployment lines, and ailing traditional industries. These are much more visible and likely to be covered by the media than are signs of entrepreneurial activity such as thousands of new small companies, new products, and new divisions in established corporations. Despite what is really happening to the economy, we are given much more evidence that it is declining than that it is changing.

Yet the appropriate policy response to changing economic conditions depends vitally on the correct diagnosis. Unemployment induced by a recession has traditionally been tackled at the federal and state levels by economic stabilization programs designed to provide temporary jobs and income until full employment returns. Unemployment caused by major structural changes may be better dealt with by measures to stimulate the birth rate of new enterprises, and policies to help the displaced to acquire the skills needed by emerging firms and to relocate to more promising areas.

Unemployment

Unemployment is the most politically volatile and closely watched economic indicator.[2] An increase in the unemployment rate is likely to increase demands for new policies to create jobs. In the late 1960s, the rate hovered around 3 percent; it has not fallen below below 7 percent since 1980. However, the increase in the average unemployment rate should be interpreted as an unambiguous indication that the economy is weaker today than it was in the 1960s.

Some unemployment is natural and efficient. "It represents the voluntary movement of persons from job to job, the movement of new entrants and reentrants into the labor force, and the process of individuals quitting their jobs to search for better employment."[3] In fact, if the quality of new job openings in a state were to improve—so that new jobs offered higher pay and better conditions—although the rate of job openings remained the same, the unemployment rate would increase as more people quit their jobs in search of better paying ones. An improvement in the state's economy would appear, statistically, as a deterioration. The rapid pace of economic development has contributed to the rising unemployment rate because of the mismatch between where plants are closing and where new firms are opening and in the skills required by new employers and those possessed by the unemployed.

The secular increase in unemployment has resulted from several other factors that have little to do with the underlying strength of the economy, including rising unemployment benefit levels, the surge of new entrants, and changing work requirements for welfare recipients.[4]

The ranks of the unemployed include many people suffering severe economic distress whose plight should be the concern of public policy. Those who have dropped out of the labor force and those involuntarily working part time are not measured by the unemployment statistic. But we cannot determine what is happening to the state economy simply by observing the unemployment rate.

Capacity Utilization

In states with a large manufacturing sector, the painful site of idle plants and unemployed workers has created the impression that development has slowed. In the early 1980s, capacity-utilization figures, such as those calculated by the Federal Reserve, suggested that a large part of the nation's productive capacity was lying idle. But the impression was misleading. The problem has been one of rapid structural change rather than slow development.

Economic capacity—how much output could be produced if resources were "fully employed"—is easier to discuss in theory than it is to measure. A shut-down, 80-year-old steel mill may be capable of producing steel, but if steel can be produced at a fraction of the cost elsewhere, that mill is not unutilized.[5] Idle capacity is not a sign of waste but an indication that, under current market conditions resources are more productively used elsewhere. If the price of steel were to increase, more plants would be brought into production and capacity would increase.[6] But, until the price of steel rises, that capacity is not excess, it is uneconomical.[7]

In addition, the capacity-utilization index suffers from an aggregation problem. "Steel" is not a homogeneous good—it comes in all types of alloys, in sheets, ingots and tubes, and many other forms. In 1981, when barely half of measured steel production capacity was in use, oil and gas wildcatters were buying tube steel from Europe and Asia because domestic producers could not meet demand. Therefore, a reported low capacity-utilization rate may signify recession, but it may also indicate rapid technological progress or a shift in demand.

Productivity Growth

Another way of measuring development has been to calculate the rate at which the productivity of the workforce has grown. This, too, has pointed to a slowdown in the rate of development during the 1970s. Between 1973 and 1983, "productivity" grew by only 0.7 percent annually, a third of the rate in the previous decade.[8] In response, some economists proposed new government initiatives to deal with the crisis of slow productivity growth.[9] Others saw less cause for alarm. Productivity statistics tend to understate the amount by which productivity is actually growing, and the combination of events that damped productivity growth in the 1970s are unlikely to recur in the coming decade.

Productivity cannot be measured directly. It is calculated by dividing national income by total paid employee hours in the private economy. There are many possibilities for error in computing national income and many pitfalls in comparing various time periods.[10] Even if output per man hour could be measured reliably, the statistic would still capture only labor and not total factor productivity, which measures how output changes in response to increases in all factors—labor, energy, raw materials, etc. For instance, total factor productivity rises when the amount of energy required to produce an automobile is reduced. But output per manhour—the conventional measure of productivity—remains unchanged.

The prospects for productivity growth in the near future are favorable. Capital investments and expenditures for research and development are rising. Even more important, many of the factors that slowed productivity growth in the 1970s have reversed themselves or been overcome:

- First, the rapid growth of the labor force, double the rate in the 1960s, necessitated much more training and encouraged firms to adopt labor intensive methods of production—raising the productivity of all other factors and slowing the growth in productivity of labor. During the next decade, labor force growth will slow.[11]
- Second, the tenfold increase in energy costs between 1973 and 1985 depressed labor productivity by encouraging the substi-

tution of labor for energy and inducing investments in energy-saving technology. People were hired to seek out ways to conserve energy, and long-term investments were made to produce fuel-efficient vehicles. Energy prices have been steady or falling in recent years, and the prospects for a comparable increase in fuel prices in the future are remote.

- Third, during the 1970s businesses made large investments in pollution control equipment to comply with new regulations. Although these investments improved the quality of the environment, they required staffing and maintenance and did not necessarily increase output. Pollution control investments are unlikely to absorb as large a portion of private investment in coming decades.

Financial Performance

Misleading conclusions also have been drawn from financial statistics. The inflation-adjusted value of shares traded on the New York Stock Exchange increased only 9 percent during the decade beginning in 1973.[12] Many Fortune 500 firms suffered record losses and layoffs, and a few declared bankruptcy. But the dismal track record of large corporations that depressed the overall stock indices is not indicative of the overall financial performance of the nation's businesses. The New York Stock Exchange index measures what is happening to America's larger, traded firms, not what is happening to new and small businesses.

An index compiled by **Venture Economics** magazine of the stock value of 100 new corporations rose from 100 in 1973 to 530 in 1984, a highly respectable 7 percent *annual* growth rate after adjustments for inflation. Venture capital corporations averaged a 25 percent rate of return on investments during the late 1970s and early 1980s.[13] In the midst of the 1982 recession, **INC** magazine had no difficulty finding 100 companies with sales growth rates that had exceeded 60 percent annually for the previous five years.

Jobs in the Future

The secular increase in the unemployment rate over the past decade has led to a growing concern that there will not be enough good jobs in the future to allow continued increases in living standards. The sudden slowing in labor productivity and the growth in the number of low-wage jobs relative to the number of high-wage jobs are frequently cited as evidence.[14] This belief has led to policies to preserve existing plants, particularly in the highly paid durable goods manufacturing sector, by subsidizing loans and enacting plant closing legislation (Chapter 4).

Earlier technological revolutions produced temporary unemployment and similar predictions that a class of permanently displaced and impoverished workers would be created. Although considerable short-term unemployment and suffering were experienced, the fears concerning long-term job prospects proved groundless. Today the fear is that highly paid manufacturing jobs will be replaced by low-paying service jobs. While the hardships of the unemployed steel workers in the Mahoning Valley and other areas cannot be ignored, there are reasons to believe that, overall, the quality of jobs and the quantity of jobs will provide expanding economic opportunities to most workers in the future.

First, it is clear that, although the share of GNP contributed by manufacturing is as large today as it was 30 years ago (about one-third), the share of the workforce employed in manufacturing is shrinking rapidly. Of the 20-million jobs created in the 1970s, only 5 percent were in manufacturing, and that sector's share of total employment has fallen from nearly 30 percent in 1970 to less than 20 percent in 1985. Innovations, such as robots, lead one expert to predict that within a decade all the manufactured products in the United States may be produced by only 9 percent of the workforce.[15] A similar revolution occurred in agriculture between 1910 and 1940.

It seems improbable that the expanding service sector will add only poor quality jobs. The growth in low-paying jobs in the 1970s was a response to the very rapid growth of the labor force, to the increase in inexperienced workers, and to soaring energy prices. As mentioned earlier, these conditions are unlikely to prevail during the next decade.

The notion that service-sector jobs must be low paying has also arisen from a failure to distinguish between traditional service jobs, such as retailing, transportation, and hotels, and "information sector" jobs such as teaching, accounting, banking, and computer programming (jobs that process information). Salaries in these professions exceed the average wage in manufacturing. The traditional service sector has been growing slowly while the information processing sector has grown dramatically. Forty-eight percent of all new jobs created between 1972 and 1983 were in professional, technical, and managerial fields.[16]

Lumping together all service employment leads to the mistaken conclusion that a shift from manufacturing to service employment must cause a decline in productivity and in the pace of economic development. In fact, some service sectors—communications, air transportation, and financial services—have exhibited large increases in productivity and promise to generate many highly paid jobs during the next decade.[17] Combined with the slowdown in labor-force growth, technological change promises to greatly increase real wages in the future, at least for those who can master the education and skills needed in new jobs.

Therefore, the relevant policy issue is not how to protect existing jobs but how to make it easier for people to move out of traditional jobs into new opportunities. Programs to keep people on the farm in the 1920s would have dramatically slowed the emergence of new industries and reduced the growth of economic opportunities. By focusing only on a few indicators of economic development and in the absence of an appropriate model of the economy, we have misjudged our economic environment at the state and national levels. We need to develop better ways to diagnose the state economy.

Better Indicators of the State Economy

There is no single indicator, nor even a small set of indicators, that provides an unambiguous measure of the performance of state economies.[18] Instead, each state must develop a set that best fits its particular economic structure and program needs. For example, some of the indicators that could be used to measure aspects of the state economy are:

Overall economic performance:[19] the rate of long-term (more than 12 weeks) unemployment; growth in per capita income; traditional indicators such as housing starts, vehicle registrations, and tax revenues.

Entrepreneurial Climate: Rate of new business formation and failures; venture capital placements in state; research activity at universities; over-the-counter stock issues; growth rate of the number of self-employed.

Long-Term Growth Prospects: rate of diversification of the economy during past 10 years; measures of the performance of primary and secondary schools; reduction in illiteracy rate during past 5 years; average educational attainment of workforce.

Other Aspects of a State's Wealth: infant mortality rate; change in air quality in major cities; change in water quality; poverty rate (after allowing for government transfers and in-kind benefits; crime rate for index crimes.

It is important to select indicators that give some measure of the state's capacity to adapt, not simply measures of growth. Emphasizing the importance of our ability to adapt rather than achieve a low rate of unemployment or a high rate of capacity utilization does not mean that all economic problems can be explained away or that the solutions to our economic problems lay outside the public sector. States confront very real problems, problems that may be reflected in the growing incidence of poverty, the slow rate of adaption of some sectors, and the lack of economic opportunity in many communities. These problems can be alleviated through a state development strategy. But we have done poorly in diagnosing the causes of these problems because we have not applied a suitable model of how the economy works.

ASSUMPTION 1: THE PURPOSE OF DEVELOPMENT POLICY IS TO CREATE JOBS

For most governors, creating jobs is a top priority for their development program. Comparing development policies according to their job-creating capacity provides a crude approximation of their relative attractiveness and may identify the prime beneficiaries of each program.

But we should not concentrate on jobs to the exclusion of other aspects of development. Some development projects may result in no new jobs or even a decline in employment. For example, some states have initiated programs to assist small machine tool firms to adapt to CAD/CAM technology, which will almost certainly allow them to cut their workforces.[20] Yet this technological improvement should be considered economic development.[21]

While the number of jobs created is an important aspect of a program, it is also important to look at the quality of jobs, increases in the productivity of all factors of production, and impacts on the quality of life of those affected. These outcomes are included under the broader goal of development we have outlined—wealth. Economic development based on entrepreneurship will result in more productive uses of all resources (measured by the value of final sales), not necessarily in ways of employing in the short-run all those who want to work.[22] However, policies undertaken for their capacity to create jobs will almost certainly cost jobs in the long-run.[23]

Some states have tried to require that the number of jobs be viewed favorably in determining eligibility for low interest rate loans, tenancy at subsidized rates in industrial parks, and selection for state contracts or other state development programs, all other factors being equal. Critics have argued that if two companies bidding on a state contract are similar in all respects but one claims that it will hire many more people than the other, this may be a reason not to award it the contract because the company is using obsolete technology or poor management practices.

Focusing on jobs may also lead policymakers to overlook policies that create entrepreneurial opportunities that allow people to create their own jobs. For example, reforming regulations (Chapter 4) does not directly create jobs, but may create new opportunities for people to exploit.

The Value of Jobs

Although job creation is politically important, jobs are only economically important if those holding them are making something that consumers value. A new factory that employs hundreds of people making products that cannot compete with those made by other firms does not contribute to development (although it would contribute to the welfare of those in the jobs).[24] "Consumption," as Adam Smith stated, "is the sole end and purpose of production." At the very least, programs to help the unemployed should not impede the long-run process of moving resources, including labor, to higher-valued uses.

Jobs producing goods and services that are not sufficiently valued by consumers to cover production costs will have to be subsidized by placing a tax—directly or indirectly—on other jobs. For example, the Congressional Budget Office estimates that quotas on imported steel cost users of steel about $150,000 in higher prices for each job saved in the steel industry. Preserving some jobs through a public subsidy must necessarily reduce the number of jobs elsewhere in the economy, perhaps by more than the number of jobs saved.

The value of goods or services is established by the people that buy and consume them. Critics of the market system have pointed out that it leads to the production of worthless items, such as pet rocks, while leaving some people homeless. This confuses two issues: efficiency in production, and the fairness of income distribution. Income distribution is addressed through governmental action, not private competition. If people in 1977 were prepared to spend four dollars to purchase a pet rock, then it was, in their minds, worth more than other things they could have purchased for a similar price. The homeless would not have been helped by a ban on the production and distribution of pet rocks.

There is no easy resolution to the conflict between those who seek to protect their investment or job from the consequences of economic development and those who seek to encourage development. This conflict is not the same as the traditional economic trade-off between equity and efficiency. Equity typically refers to how resources are distributed among different income groups. The political concern with distribution is sometimes, but not always, concerned with equity. It is also concerned, quite naturally, with how programs are distributed geographically (what does this mean for my district?) and with the distribution of benefits and costs among special interest groups with whom the elected official may be aligned.

A successful state development strategy must include policies that reduce the burden on those losing their jobs so that opposition to change is lessened (see chapter 6). The policies needed to negotiate this trade-off successfully will vary among states and within states over time because the relative importance of distribution and wealth creation on any given issue will vary among states, among different groups in the labor force, and among industries.

Public Projects and Jobs

Well-planned public projects contribute to the economy and create jobs in the long run. Waterfront projects in Boston and Baltimore have brought many shoppers and visitors downtown and converted previously underused land and buildings into valuable retail and office space. Water projects in the West have created valuable recreational and irrigation opportunities. But they are only valuable if the finished facility is valued by local households and businesses and, **in itself,** creates wealth. And projects will only create a net increase in wealth and employment in the long-run if they have genuine economic value. Spending money on public works, in and of itself, contributes little to the state economy. The claims of many projects for funding, however, are reinforced with the argument that their construction will create jobs.[25]

The project will, of course, create jobs in the immediate vicinity. But while these jobs are a benefit locally, they should not be counted as a "benefit" by the state (if that is the entity funding it) and even less of a benefit to the nation as a whole. It is often forgotten that the wage bill of those building the project is as much a cost to government as it is to private industry. It is not a benefit and should not be counted as a benefit when determining whether the project's benefits exceed its costs. Jobs are an impact, not a net benefit of the project.

It often appears that a major public project is creating jobs because the effects of the construction expenditures are concentrated and visible. Appearances, however, are misleading. Raising the money to pay for the project reduces employment elsewhere in the economy. Increasing taxes or borrowing to pay for construction produces an offsetting decline in output and employment because taxpayers must reduce their spending to pay the additional taxes.[26] Indeed, given the efficiency loss incurred in the collection of tax dollars, it is possible that there will be a net decline in jobs during the construction phase of the project. That does not mean that the project should not be built. It means that public infrastructure investments should only be undertaken for their long term economic value, not on the grounds that they will create jobs merely by the spending of money.

While the offsetting effects of raising taxes fall clearly within the financing jurisdiction, it may be argued that borrowing can shift the burden out of state and so create a net increase in employment. However, the debt must be serviced with higher taxes in the future, which may be anticipated in the municipal bond market and reflected in bond ratings. Even if the offset is not perfect and immediate, it will be strong.[27]

Another argument in favor of the job creating powers of public works is that the direct employment created by the project will lead to further indirect employment as the paychecks of the construction workers or, after the completion of the project, of the facility staff circulate in the local economy. However, if there is an indirect effect of spending, there must also have been an indirect effect of raising the money that more or less offsets the spending "multiplier".

The multiplier only helps identify the distributional impacts of public expenditures. This is an important consideration in the political process of project approval. It indicates where jobs are diverted by collecting taxes or borrowing and spending on the specific program. But multiplier effects do not enter into cost benefit evaluations. The multiplier cannot be used correctly to support a claim that public projects should be undertaken because they will create jobs.

If the project is paid for with grants from a higher level of government for a project, then it is valid to argue that the project may create jobs locally, at least in the short-run. However, state grants programs for localities tend to spread their funds more and more evenly over time as local officials learn the rules of grantsmanship. As a consequence, the ability of any single jurisdiction to be a net importer of state funds under any program will diminish. Also many (but certainly not all) facilities erected simply to create jobs rather than for their intrinsic value require an operating subsidy that raises local taxes and displaces other local jobs in the long-run.

ASSUMPTION 2: DEVELOPMENT PROGRAMS SHOULD BE TARGETED AT GROWTH INDUSTRIES

State resources are limited. Faced with an infinite array of potential clients, state development programs have sought to identify those firms or industries offering the best prospects for growth. The four guidelines most frequently employed to identify these growth industries are:

- Industries or firms whose output is sold outside the region or whose output is a substitute for goods imported into the region;
- Industries or firms with a very high value added (or difference between sales price and the cost of raw materials);
- Small businesses;
- High-tech firms.

These guidelines reflect important aspects of the development process but are not a reliable targeting rule.

Export or Import-Substituting Industries and Firms

As mentioned above, many state programs are aimed at expanding the state's export base—that is, increasing employment and capital formation in firms that sell goods outside the region or state. In most areas, this is reflected in special assistance to manufacturing or resource-based companies. For example, many states limit the use of Industrial Revenue Bonds to manufacturing and wholesale firms; others link property tax exemptions and abatements to the volume of investment in physical plant and equipment (which favors manufacturing over service firms); and most states limit their recruitment programs to out-of-state manufacturing firms.

This export-based policy reflects the reasonable view that employment in sectors that serve strictly local needs will only increase if the income of the community increases. Community income will only increase through the growth of those firms that sell out of state. New firms that are selling to a national market have a greater prospect for growth than those that only sell locally, and they will be less inclined to expand or contract in time with the local economy. For a local community using the proceeds from state or federal grants, a subsidy to attract an export firm may boost local development.

But export firms (or import-substitute firms) are certainly not the only way a community can create wealth, nor are they necessarily the best way. A subsidy for an export industry will not necessarily increase wealth by as much as the same subsidy spent on a local industry.[28] For example, the money spent building an industrial site for a new food processing plant could have been spent building a recreational area for local residents. Even if the latter creates fewer jobs than the former, it may be more valuable.[29]

For states as well as nations, exports are not an end in themselves but only a means of acquiring goods that would be more costly to produce domestically. Subsidizing "exporting" firms (through preferential tax treatment, low interest rate loans, or other state and local fiscal favors) has the same effect as taxing domestic production and donating the proceeds to people living outside the state's boundaries. The state's wealth is diminished as employment is shifted from domestic to export production.

Untraded goods can draw in resources from the outside and add to a community's wealth as easily as traded goods. People are free to move among areas and may be attracted by such local amenities as recreation, cultural services, and an attractive environment—all nontraded goods and services. The in-migration of well-educated and skilled people may prove to be a more powerful inducement to development than are state subsidies to export industries. Also an entrepreneur who succeeds first in the nontraded sector may go on to create new enterprises in the export sector. Dividing the local economy into traded and nontraded goods is not useful for development policy.

If states were to pursue an "export-based" strategy, they would find it difficult to identify their export industries. When economists first attempted to identify the export base, they assumed that services (transportation, finance, utilities, retail and wholesale, government, health, and education) and construction existed only to meet local demand, and that manufacturing and agriculture were the basic export sectors and this rule-of-thumb has been widely adopted. There are two reasons why this division is inappropriate.

First, a large part of the manufacturing sector may exist to meet local demands, including printing, food processing, and the production of some fabricated metals and certain types of mechanical and electrical equipment.

Second, important industries in the service sector can be export driven, even though they would be difficult for a development agency to identify in advance. Since 1980 legal services have surpassed apparel as New York City's largest export industry. In Sioux Falls, South Dakota, the largest employer is Citibank. And in Freeport, Maine, the local economy has grown rapidly as a result of the "export-driven" expansion of a local retail store, L.L. Bean.

A state government is unlikely to "pick winners" by aiming at export industries. Identifying profitable opportunities is more effectively achieved by decentralized competition among entrepreneurs than through a public development agency.

High-Value-Added Firms

States rich in natural resources have pursued "high-value-added" strategies. Anxious to diversify beyond the extractive industries, they have tried to attract firms that process the raw materials with which they are endowed. For example, Louisiana has employed tax abatements and exemptions to attract petrochemical plants to use its natural gas supplies. Firms with high value added are assumed— for the most part correctly—to offer high wages and to employ relatively skilled workers.[30]

The problems with this approach are similar to those encountered in targeting export industries: there may be many valuable wealth-creating opportunities among low value-added industries and firms. The high value-added industries may have meager growth prospects in the United States or may have input requirements that are incompatible with the state's endowments.

Small Businesses

In probably the most widely read article in the history of economic development, David Birch of MIT found that small businesses— those with fewer than 20 employees—were responsible for 80 percent of the net increase in employment between 1969 and 1976.[31] States have established numerous programs to assist small businesses, from technical assistance centers and loan programs to targeted procurement programs and one-stop regulatory agencies. Unfortunately, a concentration on small business per se overlooks an important point. Small businesses are less important than new businesses in shaping state development. While many new businesses start small, the emphasis for development policy should be on the formation of new enterprises regardless of size and not on small businesses regardless of age.

For the past fifteen years, the national economy has generated about two million jobs annually—a rate far in excess of any other developed country (except Canada). New, not small, businesses were responsible for half these jobs. These two-million new jobs were the net result of the loss of four-million existing jobs offset by the creation of six-million new ones.[32] During an average year, two-million people lost their jobs when the firms employing them reduced their payrolls, and another two-million jobs were lost in firms that went out of business. Offsetting these losses, three-million jobs were created in brand new businesses and through the additional hiring of three-million people by existing firms. Most of this occurred in either the branch plants of large businesses or in a few small entrepreneurial companies that experience rapid changes in employment from year to year.

In any state, these ratios may differ somewhat—growth areas tend to enjoy a higher birth rate of new firms, for example. But in all states, job loss and job creation are part of the same process. Few jobs in any state or region—at most 3 or 4 percent—are created or lost as a result of business relocation.

As the pace of economic change has accelerated, the importance of new businesses in creating jobs has grown, despite a sharp recession. The annual rate of business formation has tripled from about 200,000 in 1970 to more than 600,000 in 1984.

The spurt in entrepreneurial activity since 1975 has been accompanied by an increase in the business failure rate. This is to be expected. New firms are experimenting with new products, processes, and markets and lack the financial resources of established companies. A high rate (per 1,000 existing businesses) of failure usually indicates a healthy rate of new business formation and not an underlying economic malaise. Nor is a low rate a healthy sign. In 1975 the business-failure rate in New York City, then in the depths of a deep recession, was lower than that in booming Houston.[33] The failure rate is an ambiguous indicator. States can gain much fuller pictures of what is happening to their economies by concentrating less on the overall rate of job growth and more on measures of entrepreneurial activity such as the rate of new business formation.

Another notable recent trend is the rapid growth in people creating their own jobs, either through self-employment or setting up a new business. Today one person in six in the labor force is either heading a business or self-employed.[34] Nearly one new job in four is either as the head of a business or in self-employment—more than double the share ten years ago. By comparison, employment in **Fortune** 1000 companies, accounting for more than 40 percent of all current jobs, actually declined over the last decade.[35]

In summary, targeting on small business may not prove useful. It is much more important to focus on the business-formation process. New businesses—many of which are small, are the most important single category of firms in the process of job generation.

High Technology

Shrinking employment among traditional industries has led some
states to pursue high-tech firms as a source of employment for their
manufacturing workforces. They are unlikely to succeed in this en-
deavor. The entire high-tech industry today accounts for 3 percent of
the workforce and is anticipated to increase its share to no more
than 4 percent by the end of the century. One new job in 25 will be
in high-tech industries.[36]

Less than half of the jobs in high technology are well paid and
require advanced skills. The majority are unskilled production and
clerical jobs that, as Atari has demonstrated, can easily move overseas.

Five states, California, Massachusetts, New York, New Jersey,
and Texas, account for 60 percent of all high-tech jobs. Others are
unlikely to be able to replicate the research infrastructure of these
states—a necessary but not sufficient condition for concentrated
high-tech development. States establishing an attractive entrepreneurial climate will stimulate the birth of new enterprises regardless of technology. Targeting high-tech will simply penalize
those who are not in favored industries.

ASSUMPTION 3: INDUSTRIAL RECRUITMENT AND RETENTION SHOULD BE THE FOCUS OF STATE EFFORTS

One common state response to the political pressure to "create jobs"
for new entrants to the labor force or for those rendered jobless as
older industries decline has been to create industrial recruitment or
retention programs. States attempt to lure industry from outside
their borders, compete for a new branch plant, or retain their existing firms with financial inducements.[37] In reality, these programs do
not improve the entrepreneurial environment and provide only
short-run benefits.

Competing states offer lavish inducements to footloose firms
and to firms considering setting up new branches:

> [One] state would build a $10 million rail spur and a $15
> million highway extension to serve the (new) plant. It would
> provide the auto company with $40 million in a 1 3/4 per-
> cent long term loan to finance the plant's completion, and a
> $3 million subsidy to train ... workers. A state teacher's and
> worker's pension fund would provide another $6 million in

loans for construction while the plant was finished, local governments would allow millions of dollars worth of tax abatements. For the first two years [the company] should be given a 95 percent tax abatement; in the next three years, 50 percent.

Robert Goodman (1980, p.2)

the bidding finally peaked with an unbeatable offer... including $30 million in faculty endowments at the [state] university, $37 million in equipment and operating expenses, $20 million worth of office space, subsidized home mortgages for micro-electronics company's employees, a petty cash fund of a half-million dollars for country club initiation fees and other services, and a Lear jet with two pilots available at all times.

Governor Bruce Babbitt (1984,p.43)

Inducing firms to relocate or to open branch plants instate has been a popular state policy. In the last decade, it has been extended to business retention as well as attraction. The approach has several attractive features:

- The successes are highly visible. Elected officials can be photographed at ground-breaking ceremonies and claim to have created employment.
- Some of the costs can be hidden. Tax expenditures (special abatements and exemptions from state and local taxes) are not reported by most states[38] and are not subject to annual budgetary review. Only California prepares an annual tax-expenditure budget that is presented to the legislature in the same way as the capital and expenditure budgets.
- Part of the costs of the inducements can be passed on to the federal taxpayer by using tax-exempt financing.[39]
- An industrial recruitment program is simple to design and implement.
- The benefits accrue to a small, well-organized constituency while the costs are dispersed over a much larger and less well-organized group.
- There is a plausible economic logic underlying the strategy.[40]

These programs seemed relatively successful during the 1940s and 1950s when companies were opening new branches and relocating. For states like Mississippi, with little industrial base to begin with, recruitment may have offered the only hope of catching up with their industrialized neighbors. But as competition to recruit firms has intensified, the growth of manufacturing has slowed, and national employment growth has depended increasingly on small new businesses and service firms. Recruitment has been less able to respond to the public's demand for jobs and income.

A closer look at the logic of offering companies tax abatements and exemptions reveals why they are not always as useful as their supporters claim:

Subsidies are not an important determinant of location decisions. In selecting a location for a new or expanding enterprise, managers look not only at taxes and other financial subsidies but at a host of other factors, including wages, labor-force skills, energy cost and reliability, access to communications and transportation, the fiscal strength of state and local governments, and the quality of life. State and local taxes rarely comprise more than 3 or 4 percent of value added, especially for new and growing firms. Low taxes are usually an indication of low levels or poor quality of public services. While inducements may not really matter, most firms, quite rationally, claim that they do matter if asked by state officials.[41]

In a survey reported in 1981, economist Michael Kieschnick reported that only half of all firms opening a new branch were even aware of the tax incentives offered by the state in which they located the branch, and business taxes were listed as the least important factor after markets, access to raw materials, and labor costs.

At least one journalist has reported that the much courted MicroComputer Corporation struck a California city from consideration when it promised not to raise taxes, reasoning that without a tax increase it would be unable to improve the quality of local schools.

One firm's subsidy is another firm's tax burden. Heavily recruited firms are offered expensive inducements whose costs must be met through service cuts or by increased taxes on existing firms and residents. In addition, if local personal taxes do not reflect the full cost of public services used by residents, then relocating workers and their families from the recruited company[42] will demand additional school facilities, water capacity, and waste treatment, forcing current residents to pay higher taxes.

There is no guarantee that the new firm will remain competitive—many have moved on to even lower-cost locations in the Caribbean or Asia.[43] It is very difficult to assess the long-run viability of a firm. Few recruitment programs make inducements conditional upon job creation, sales growth, or other measures of success. Therefore, the state's tax incidence is tilted away from incoming firms, regardless of their contribution to the local economy and toward local firms. This will dampen development among indigenous firms and entrepreneurs.

Recruitment programs weaken the state's entrepreneurial climate. In recent years, states' efforts to attract MCC and General Motor's Saturn plant have been widely publized. But by and large, the type of firms that respond to financial inducements are those with low profit margins, are the least innovative, and make no investments in the skills of their employees. For example, textile and apparel firms in southern states have been recruited under development programs. These firms are usually branches of major corporations and can calculate production costs accurately. Once established, these branches do not grow, undertake research, or introduce innovative products or production methods. And they provide none of the environment necessary to support entrepreneurial development. Spin-off new businesses are rare.

The persisting popularity of recruitment programs demonstrates the conflict between programs aimed at creating jobs in the short-run and the actions that are necessary to form the environment needed to create wealth and jobs in the long-run. Recruitment may bring new business to a state, but economic development cannot wait for a successful recruiting expedition. For most states, willing recruits are few and far between. The additional costs imposed on a state's businesses and residents to make up for the recruited firm's abatements and exemptions discourage risk-taking and dampen the search for more productive ways to use resources. The beguiling logic of the programs and their apparent successes, however, have ensured them a permanent place in states' development strategies.

IMPLICATIONS FOR STATE DEVELOPMENT POLICY

There are several important lessons to be learned from this review of traditional state development policies. The first is that by trying to diagnose our economic environment through relying on a few popular economic indicators may present a misleading picture. The unemployment rate, capacity utilization, productivity growth, financial indicators, and other widely used measures of performance only tell part of the story. They show nothing of the level of entrepreneurial activity occurring in the state and therefore do not distinguish between a slowing in the rate of growth and an acceleration in the rate of change. The process of diagnosing the state economy must be based upon a wider and different set of indicators, and interpretation should be based on the economic development process outlined in the preceding chapter.

Second, how well a program appears to create jobs is a poor way to select them for inclusion in the state's economic development strategy. Public works projects should be undertaken for their long term value, not because of their capacity to create jobs. Industry targeting is also misleading and may lead a state to ignore valuable investments in untargeted industries. Neither exporting firms, high-value-added or high technology industry, nor small business is an appropriate target for development strategies because entrepreneurial opportunities for wealth creation exist in all sectors and cannot be identified in the process of policy analysis.

Third, recruitment and retention programs based upon discretionary subsidies to specific firms are rarely cost-effective. These programs tend to emphasize subsidies for large-scale capital investment—not entrepreneurship—and to emphasize attracting firms and branch plants from out of state rather than to encourage new business formation. While states must establish that they are not "antibusiness," a focus exclusively upon larger firms only draws upon a small part of the economic potential of the state.

Programs to promote the state by providing information about its advantages to industry must remain a part of every state's strategy. For a state to fail to advertise its merits may convey a difficult and antibusiness environment. But these promotional efforts should be limited to the distribution of information and should not include distortions of the tax code.

Finally, current development policies mobilize only a small part of states' resources. Education, regulatory powers, public works, and many other state activities are carried out with little thought for their effect on development. We cannot begin to develop more effective state policies until we have established what is needed to create an environment for sustained entrepreneurship.

NOTES

1. Data from the Bureau of the Census, **Census of Governments, 1982,** Washington, D.C., U.S. Department of Commerce, 1984. State development agencies represent very little net expenditure. For example, most agencies issuing tax exempt bonds to finance private investment in plant and equipment cover their operating expenses and require no state appropriation.

2. The unemployment rate is compiled from a survey of 60,000 households. The unemployed are those who did not work during the survey week but made efforts during the prior four weeks to find a job by registering with unemployment agencies or writing job applications. The United States' measure of unemployment is much less rigorous than that used in European countries, which may count only those who formally report at a government agency. U.S. rates cannot be compared with European rates without adjusting the data.

3. Clarkson and Mieners, 1979, p.45.

4. The rapid inflow of young and female workers into the labor force meant that newcomers searched longer for employment (see Cagan, 1977 and Flaim, 1979).

   Increases in the real value of unemployment benefits since 1970 have meant that people could afford to hold out longer when searching for a job (see Ehrenberg and Oaxaca, 1976). This has led to a better match-up between people and jobs, which may improve productivity. This is reflected in a higher rate, which is usually interpreted as an unambiguously bad sign.

   Work registration requirements for welfare, foodstamps, and public training programs have drawn many people into the ranks of the unemployed who were not counted in the 1960s (Clarkson and Meiners, 1979). This does not argue that these people should not be counted, only that they have been "added" to the measured ranks of the unemployed between 1970 and 1980, creating the impression that conditions have worsened.

5. For example, corn can be grown in residential backyards and would be if the price of corn were to reach very high levels. However, backyards are not counted as idle capacity when we measure the nation's capacity for growing corn. We should be similarly suspicious of measures that include obsolete steel mills.

6. If in 1982, when some indices showed the U.S. steel industry operating at about 40 percent of "capacity," we had eliminated from consideration all plants older than the oldest Japanese mill, the capacity utilization rate would have been closer to 100 percent. Far from being troubled by excess capacity, the steel industry has too little capacity that can be used economically (see **Iron Age Magazine,** various issues).

7. In addition, the capacity utilization index suffers from an aggregation problem. "Steel" is not a homogeneous good—it comes in all types of alloys, in sheets, ingots and tubes, and many other forms. In 1981, when barely half of measured steel production capacity was in use, oil and gas wildcatters were buying tube steel from Europe and Asia because domestic producers could not meet demand.

8. Kendrick, 1984.

9. See Thurow, 1980, Magaziner and Reich, 1982, and Rohatyn, 1984.

10. See Winter, 1980. If the same number of man hours are required to produce an automobile in 1983 as in 1973, does this mean that productivity has not increased. If less energy and materials are used, then total productivity has increased. And since the 1983 model car gets better fuel mileage, emits less pollution, requires less maintenance, and is safer, then—after adjusting for quality—labor productivity has also increased.

11. See Winter, 1984. The 16-24 age group will actually decline in absolute size, raising productivity growth.

12. Levine, 1984.

13. See **Venture Economics,** various issues.

14. See Bluestone and Harrison, 1983, Ginsburg, 1977, and Gordon, 1981.

15. **Economist,** July 28, 1984.

16. Serrin, 1984.

17. Rukeyser, 1984.

18. This issue is dealt with in greater detail in Pollard et al., forthcoming.

19. Some people have tried to relate the pace of economic development and the causes of unemployment to the slow rate of growth of productivity (Thurow, 1980). Between 1973 and 1983, "productivity" grew by only 0.7 percent annually, a third of the rate in the previous decade (Hendrick, 1984). In response, some economists proposed new government initiatives to deal with the crisis of slow productivity growth (Thurow, 1980, Magaziner and Reich, 1982). Others see less cause for alarm. Productivity statistics tend to understate the amount by which productivity is actually growing, and the combination of events that dampened productivity growth in the 1970s is unlikely to recur in the coming decade.

20. CAD/CAM is Computer Assisted Design/Computer Assisted Manufacturing technology that greatly simplifies the process of calibrating machine tools.

21. There are many other examples in which considerations other than the number of jobs are important when evaluating development programs. Occupants of an industrial park, for example, should be selected with some concern over the quality of jobs they offer and their environmental impacts. Job quality would include some measure of the stability of employment, wage level, opportunities for promotion, and other factors. State investments in technology development would be based upon the expected value of new technologies, independent of the number of jobs created or saved.

22. The conflict between creating wealth and preserving the jobs of those displaced is greatest when the new jobs being created by entrepreneurial action are not located near the jobs that are being destroyed (in Silicon Valley rather than the Mahoning Valley), and when the skills required in new jobs are very different from those possessed by the unemployed (electronics engineers rather than steel workers).

23. Some states have attempted to require that the number of jobs be viewed favorably in determining eligibility for low interest rate loans, tenancy at subsidized rates in industrial parks, selection for state contracts or other state development programs all other factors being equal. Critics have argued that if two companies bidding on a state contract are similar in all respects but one claims that it will hire many more people than the other, this may be probably a reason not to award it the contract since it is using obsolete technology or poor management practices.

24. Jobs whose product is not sufficiently valued by consumers to cover production costs will have to be subsidized by placing a tax—directly or indirectly—on other jobs. For example, the Congressional Budget Office estimates that quotas on imported steel cost users of steel about $150,000 in higher prices for each job saved in the steel industry. Preserving some jobs through a public subsidy must necessarily reduce the number of jobs elsewhere in the economy perhaps by more than the number of jobs saved.

25. There are many examples of this type of argument. Most applications for Urban Development Action Grants include, as benefits, induced employment. Most cost benefit studies of Bureau of Reclamation and Corps of Engineers water projects add jobs created through a multiplier effect as a benefit.

26. It might be argued that the taxpayers' spending would have been on commodities purchased from out of state, and that spending their money in state will create jobs. But a very large share of construction spending is for material that, for most states, will come from out of state, and construction labor is much more likely to be temporarily imported than labor in other industries because of its rigidly demarcated skills (Vernez et al., 1977).

The most famous example of an economist arguing that an increase in public spending would create jobs is British economist John Maynard Keynes (in **General Theory of Money, Interest and Employment,** Oxford: Oxford University Press, 1936, Book III, p.129) who said:

> If the Treasury were to fill old bottles with banknotes, bury them at suitable depths in disused coalmines which are then filled up to the surface with town rubbish, and leave it to private enterprise on well-tried principles of laissez-faire to dig the notes up again ... there need be no more unemployment and, with the help of the repercussions, the real income of the community, and its capital wealth also, would probably become a good deal greater than it actually is.

His argument has passed into many textbooks and economic models. However, Keynes was considering a special case in which the government was able to draw upon idle funds that were not about to be either spent or invested. This special case is of no relevance when considering public actions today.

27. Recent work on rational expectations suggests that the offset will be very similar whether taxes or borrowing is used (Barro, 1985).

28. The addition to the wealth of a community created by the increase in output in the export firm is the sum of: the net value of the new jobs (i.e. the difference between the price at which the individual was willing to work and the actual wage, plus the increase in the net value of the firm pro-rated to local shareholders.

29. Local preferences affect the values of nontraded goods relative to traded goods— they cannot influence the prices of traded goods very much.

30. Petroleum refining and petrochemicals have the highest value added per employee of all industries at the two-digit level of Standard Industrial Classification (SIC). Value added is the difference between gross sales and the cost of raw materials.

31. See Birch 1978 and 1980.

32. Armington and Odle, 1982. The contribution of small and new businesses to the job creation process has been one of the most controversial development issues in recent years. In a widely publized study, David Birch (1978 and 1981) concluded that small businesses contributed 80 percent of the new jobs created between 1968 and 1976. These results were disputed by Catherine Armington and Marjorie Odle (1982) who, using the Dun and Bradstreet credit files for different years (but employing a different technical method for preparing the files), concluded that small businesses accounted for only 40 percent of new jobs and new business more than 50 percent. The complex statistical issues underlying this dispute are discussed in Schweke and Friedman, 1982.

33. See Dun and Bradstreet reports on business failures monthly. The failure rate is a highly unreliable statistic. A failure will only show up on Dun and Bradstreet files if there is a credit inquiry about the firm. A business that quietly folds up and pays off creditors may not show up as having failed for several years and firms that are restructured under a new name and new management may show up as failures.

34. See data in **The State of Small Business,** U.S. Small Business Administration, Washington D.C., 1983 and **Employment and Training Report of the President,** U.S. Department of Labor, various years.

35. Shrinking employment among larger companies does not necessarily imply that their sales were declining or that they were experiencing difficulties. Increased

productivity, contracting out, and shifting jobs overseas also reduced domestic hiring.

36. There are many different definitions of high technology —see Joint Economic Committee, 1982; Riche et al., 1983. The numbers presented here are from **Business Week,** March 28, 1983 and **The New York Times,** October 14, 1984, Educational Supplement.

37. The Urban Institute prepared the following list of popular state development tools:

FINANCIAL INCENTIVES
Grants
Loans
Interest Subsidies
Direct Subsidies
Loan Guarantees
Industrial Revenue Bonds
General Revenue Bonds
Umbrella Bonds
Equity and Near-equity Financing
Tax Incentives

NONFINANCIAL ASSISTANCE
Business Consulting
Management Training
Market Studies
Site Selection
Streamlined Licensing, Regulation, and Permitting
Customized Job Training
Research and Development
Business Procurement Assistance
Specialty Services

IMPROVEMENTS IN BUSINESS ENVIRONMENT
Physical Environment
Public Infrastructure Development
Land Banking
Speculative Buildings
Business Councils and Economic Development Corporations
Source: **Directory of Incentives for Business Investment Decisions in the United States.** Washington D.C.: The Urban Institute, 1983.

38. Only California prepares an annual tax-expenditure budget that is presented to the legislature in the same way as the capital and expenditure budgets.

39. Mississippi, the state that invented smokestack chasing in the 1930s, invented the Industrial Revenue Bond at the same time.

40. The logic supporting industrial recruitment programs is that new firms will create jobs that will expand the state and local tax base, justifying the initial forgiveness of taxes. In addition, these enterprises create further local jobs through a multiplier effect. The way to attract firms is to offer them inducements that reduce the cost of doing business in the state.

41. In a survey reported in 1981, Michael Kieschnick reported that only half of all firms opening a new branch were even aware of the tax incentives offered by the state in which they located the branch, and business taxes were listed as the least important factor after markets, access to raw materials, and labor costs.

42. Some studies have found that as many as 50 percent of the jobs in a company migrating into a state are filled by people who follow that company into the state (Vaughan, 1977).

43. In the first example of recruiting inducements, cited above, the auto plant is operating at less than half its capacity, and the parent company is considering shutting it down. The second case is still too new to predict its long-run prospects.

CHAPTER 4

THE ENTREPRENEURIAL ENVIRONMENT

The entrepreneurial spirit, the potential for discovery, is always waiting to be released. Human ingenuity is irrepressible and perennial; and to release it requires an environment free from special privilege or blockages against new numbers.

Israel Kirzner (1984, p.57)

British taxpayers provided the funds and Nobel prize-winning scientists at Cambridge University added the genius that led to the development of monoclonal antibodies—a major advance in genetic engineering. But the primary economic benefits of this discovery were harvested not by the British but by southern Californians whose firms are developing the commercial applications of this new technology. One reason for this emigration of economic development is that Great Britain lacks the entrepreneurial environment to convert new ideas into commercially viable products and processes.[1]

Potential entrepreneurs exist in all communities, no matter what their level of development or system of government.[2] Whether they emerge depends upon the environment for entrepreneurship: Are there obstacles to the pursuit of opportunity? Are there incentives for risk-taking? Few entrepreneurial stories unfold as an effortless journey from conception to market. The entrepreneurial environment will influence how many entrepreneurs embark on this journey and how many succeed.

The process of wealth creation is complex. It requires the coordination of many different types of resources: entrepreneurs must be able to acquire information and advice; communicate their project to potential backers; overcome technical, production, and managerial obstacles; and finally persuade customers to try their products. Employees must be able to find out about alternative employment opportunities. Investors must evaluate alternative investment projects.

Many elements define the environment for entrepreneurship; this chapter describes the role that state government activities play in establishing a competitive environment. The cost and availability of the capital needed to make investments in plant and equipment, human skills, and public infrastructure are vitally important and are discussed in Chapters 5, 6, and 7 respectively.

51

Other government activities also influence the entrepreneurial environment. In pursuing its many different and often conflicting objectives—consumer protection, environmental protection, public safety and health, equal opportunity, and welfare of the poor— governments have legislated and regulated many aspects of economic life. Some of these measures limit entrepreneurial activity by restricting entry into certain trades, professions, and industries, and by limiting the ability of firms to compete for consumer spending (by setting price and quality levels, for example). These restrictions are discussed in the first section of this chapter.

Regulations should not be abandoned solely because they have an adverse impact on entrepreneurs. But state policy makers must seek ways of reforming regulatory policies so that they achieve the goals of the regulations without unnecessarily restricting entrepreneurial incentives. The political obstacles to doing this, however, are often acute. The first section also shows how some groups come to profit from state actions that influence economic activity and will oppose the repeal and reform of the regulations from which they benefit.

Finally, the social attitude toward entrepreneurship is important. Is "new money" frowned upon? Is business failure a stigma?[3] Are entrepreneurial role models looked upon favorably? These aspects are discussed in the final section.

BARRIERS TO ENTREPRENEURSHIP

New York City requires a medallion for each taxicab operating in the city. There are 11,772 medallions, and no new medallions have been issued since 1937. Today a medallion sells for $80,000—a measure of the monopoly enjoyed by medallion owners.[4] The result is higher fares for riders, absence of service in low-income neighborhoods (which means fewer jobs as cab drivers for residents of those neighborhoods), and poorly maintained and unsafe cabs.[5] The city's Taxi and Limousine Commission continues to bend to the wishes of medallion owners and has not expanded the number of medallions.

By contrast, cabs in Washington, D.C., must pay less than $100 for a license to operate, and there are no limits to the number of cabs. Most of the cabs are owner operated, not fleets as in New York. Costs per passenger mile are much lower (and accidents much fewer), and there are 12 cabs per 1,000 people in D.C. compared with only 2.5 per 1,000 in New York. Several cities have deregulated, including San

Diego, and data suggest that prices are reduced, consumer satisfaction increased, and the availability of rides expanded.[6]

The first requirement for a healthy entrepreneurial environment is the opportunity to compete. Yet entrepreneurs face widespread barriers to pursuing opportunities that are the result of government legislation and regulation. In theory, large economies of scale and collusion among firms can also create barriers to entry.[7] However, economies of scale are more important in theory than in practice, and in the absence of coercion, collusion among firms cannot exclude newcomers or repress innovation for long.

For the most part, these barriers to entrepreneurship have not arisen deliberately, yet neither have they survived by accident. Typically they were introduced to protect consumers from physical harm and poor quality products and services. For example, educational institutions are accredited by state agencies to protect people from the "diploma mills" that sprang up when the G.I. Bill was enacted after World War II; usury laws were introduced to protect people against loan sharks; state examinations are required of beauticians so that people will not receive poor quality or dangerous treatment; and truck loading regulations were adopted to make roads safer.

Other regulations have been adopted to protect jobs instate. For example, out-of-state agricultural produce must often pass much higher quality standards than home-grown produce before it can be sold in state; professional certification in one state is not recognized in another; and in-state firms receive preferential treatment when bidding on state contracts.

Alfred Kahn, head of the Civil Aeronautics Board under President Jimmy Carter and an expert on government regulation, summarized how economic regulations end up limiting competition (1984, p. 8):

> But the common characteristic of strictly economic regulation, wherever it is practiced, is that it not only substitutes for competition in situations where competition is infeasible or inadequately protects the public, it proceeds by suppressing competition; it restricts the entry of rivals, divides up markets, and obstructs and, typically, flatly prohibits price competition among firms in the industry.

Once enacted, restrictions develop a dependent clientele so that, even if the conditions that gave rise to the restriction change or if a better way to achieve the same goals is found, the firms and individuals who benefit from it fight to retain it. For example, New York medallion holders fight to maintain the limit on medallions because theirs would fall in value if additional medallions were issued; lawyers oppose state recognition of out-of-state certification; and borrowers with low interest rate loans oppose any relaxation in usury ceilings. It is particularly difficult to change such regulations because the benefits are usually highly concentrated and often large enough to make investments in lobbying worthwhile. The costs—which may include higher prices and poorer quality service for consumers, fewer opportunities for potential entrepreneurs, and an overall environment inhibiting to entrepreneurs—are usually widespread, yet are too small for each individual to make counterlobbying worthwhile.

As well intentioned as the original justifications may seem, and as carefully as the legislation was designed, current regulations can be repealed or reformed without jeopardizing the objectives for which they were introduced. The changing economic environment and experimentation by different states have produced ways of achieving this. Identifying these opportunities requires a careful analysis of the economics of the occupation or industry involved and of the effects of past regulatory efforts. It also requires careful analysis of the politics of regulatory reform. The following subsections briefly suggest where opportunities may exist for removing barriers to entrepreneurial activity.

Publicly Created Barriers to Entry and Exit

States have passed many laws limiting the ability of people to enter occupations and businesses. Many of these regulations originate at the local level, but the power to make these regulations has been bestowed on localities, explicitly or implicitly, by states.

More than 500 occupations are protected by entry restrictions, which include a limited number of apprenticeship openings and nonrecognition of out-of-state qualifications. One study estimates that these restrictions—reflected in 2,800 state laws—increase the earnings of protected professionals by 12 percent, while another study documents how these restrictions have been used to exclude minorities from well-paying professional jobs.[8]

States also regulate entry into many industries. Fear of bank failures has led to extensive federal and state regulations governing the banking industry.[9] New entrants are required to prove to the state that there is a demand for their services before they can go into business. The result is higher prices and more limited services. The rapidly changing structure of the financial sector should encourage states to review their regulations. The health-care industry is also tightly constrained because of state concern that the massive expansion of Medicaid and Medicare will lead to overbuilding and inflated costs. Dissatisfaction with the results of current regulatory practices has led to a more entrepreneurial approach.[10]

In most states, the rapidly emerging telecommunications sector is subject to extensive and chaotic regulation. For example, states allow cities to grant a multiyear monopoly to a cable TV company in return for the company laying the network.[11] The result has been slow exploitation of the potential of cable communications systems and dampened innovation. Cities were reluctant to encourage more competition initially because they felt that, without a formal monopoly, the cable company would not lay the basic cable network (this is allowed under the federal Cable Communications Act of 1984 as well as by most states). Later they maintained the monopoly because they were unwilling to forgo the tax revenues that franchisers are able to pay.[12]

Economic development cannot occur unless resources move from industries that are declining to those that are expanding. Barriers to exit prevent this shift by freezing resources in less-productive uses. For example, requiring firms to give advance notice and to make separation payments may raise the cost of labor to the firm and discourage hiring. Firms will be reluctant to add new workers if they believe that increases in sales are only temporary. Forcing firms to operate facilities that are suffering losses prevents those resources from flowing to uses where they will be more valued.

There are more effective ways for states to assist individuals displaced by economic development (Chapter 6) without preventing firms from closing or forcing them to compensate released workers.

Limiting Competition

To protect consumers, states limit the ability of enterprises to set their own prices: some states impose usury ceilings on consumer loans, most states regulate health-care prices, and some allow municipalities to regulate the housing rents, mass transit, and telecommunications services. The consequences of these laws are often quite different from those intended.

Usury laws, intended to protect consumers from excessive interest charges, have not kept down interest rates but have instead denied credit to groups that would have benefited from borrowing. Riskier borrowers, which include many low-income people, are the first to be excluded from credit markets when interest rates paid elsewhere exceed the state limits. The poor are effectively denied the opportunity to finance investments in vehicles, homes, businesses, and certain types of education.

States regulate almost all aspects of the agricultural sector, setting marketing prices, providing credit, inspecting harvests, and setting quality standards. Some regulations are intended to protect harvests from disease and infestation, some to protect consumers from poor quality produce, and some to protect farmers from out-of-state competition. In 11 western states alone, researchers Steven Craig and Joel Sailors from the University of Houston found 1,500 restrictions on interstate agricultural trade.[13] They estimated that the nationwide effect of such restraints may cost consumers $150 billion annually in higher prices, only a part of which is offset by higher incomes earned by farmers. Fixing prices and sometimes the quality of the product sold, guaranteeing a market, and regulating production quantities have eroded many of the incentives that typically stimulate enterprise and innovation.

Finally, most state tax codes reflect the relative power of established industries and place new firms at a competitive disadvantage. Large branch plants enjoy tax abatements and exemptions that were given for moving into the state (Chapter 3). Established industries have been given special deductions, allowances, and provisions to retain them in state and in recognition of their political and economic importance. Some of those that may have threatened to leave may have been given special subsidies: a state-provided facility, a low interest rate loan, or a special training program for its workforce.

THE ENTREPRENEURIAL TRADITION

The most important single factor in the rise of a "Silicon Valley" is entrepreneurial fever. It is doubtful that its spirit can be taught in formal classes, although several universities now have courses on entrepreneurship. Entrepreneurship is best learned by example. When individuals know of successful role models like Steve Jobs, Bob Noyce, Bill Hewlett, Dave Packard, and Nolan Bushnell, they naturally begin to think, "If he did it, why can't I?" Once an entrepreneurial climate becomes established in an area like Silicon Valley, individuals seek work there in order to step into an entrepreneurial role. Entrepreneurial fever is concentrated in an area both by modeling and by selective migration.

Rogers and Larsen (1984, p.234)

There are vast differences in entrepreneurial activity among communities and among states, not all of which can be explained by differences in artificial barriers. Some areas, most notably Silicon Valley, California, have developed a strong entrepreneurial tradition that encourages development. The deep pool of talent found in the valley attracts and develops new talent. This tradition was not created by recruiting large firms and hiring MBAs from elsewhere:

> Most communities and states attempting to establish a scientific complex seek transplanting growth and appear to be ignorant of the importance of growth from within through the formation of new firms. Instead of trying to seduce other cities' companies, officials wanting to start a high-technology complex should be thinking about their own spin-offs. But a steady stream of city, state, and national officials come to Silicon Valley, seeking to woo California firms to their area by offering tax breaks, cheap land, and other inducements. Most of these trips are futile.
>
> An agglomeration of spin-offs in the same neighborhood as their parent firms is why a high-technology complex builds up in a certain region. The chain reaction of spin-offs from spin-offs is a kind of natural process, once it has begun. Setting off the initial spark is the key.
>
> Rogers and Larsen (1984, p.235)

In contrast, those states or communities that have been dominated for decades by a single industry or firm paying high wages have not had the opportunity to develop an entrepreneurial tradition. The incentive to start up a business is dampened by high wages (and high lay-off benefits). In those places where traditional employers have closed plants and reduced workforces, the absence of an entrepreneurial tradition has led the community to reject entrepreneurship as a development policy. But if the unemployed recognize that former employers will not return, they will be prime candidates to become entrepreneurs. The opportunity cost of starting a new business is lower for the unemployed than for those working (Chapter 8). Albert Shapero summarizes the importance of these disruptions as stimulants for new enterprise formation (1981, p.22):[14]

> A study of 109 company formations in Austin, Texas, for example, found that 65 percent of the influences leading to the startup of new companies were negative. The influences identified included 'getting fired,' 'boss sold the company,' 'organizational changes,' 'being transferred but did not want to leave the city,' 'no future,' and 'didn't like the job.'

The more strongly people are protected from the consequences of change—by public subsidies to declining industries and other policies—the less incentive they have to respond when economic transformation can no longer be resisted.

Entrepreneurial activity is normally associated with individuals and small firms. Individuals, working alone or in small firms, have been responsible for more than half of the major inventions of the twentieth century, including the airplane, automatic transmission, and the personal computer.[15] Small firms are also responsible for a much larger share of important innovations than their share of employment or research and development expenditure would predict.[16] By one estimate, firms with fewer than 100 employees produced 24 times as many process innovations per research dollar than firms employing more than 1,000 people.[17] Large organizations, both public and private, which may be good at managing large-scale, repetitive operations, are perceived as being less entrepreneurial than smaller ones.

Entrepreneurship, however, is not limited to new or small enterprises. Many large firms have performed well in a dynamic economic environment by creating environments that harness the entrepreneurial energies of their workforces. The most important factors are encouraging competition and rewarding individual initiative.

As long as risk-taking is encouraged and successful innovation is rewarded, firms can encourage entrepreneurial behavior among their workforce even after they grow large.[18] An Wang, founder of the office machine firm with annual sales exceeding two billion dollars, instructed his staff: "Take risks. I want you to feel free to try things, even if they fail. If you do the same thing twice, I'll figure you had a new twist. If you do it a third time, I'll fire you".[19]

Minnesota Mining and Manufacturing (3M), developer of the Post-it Notes described in Chapter 2, operates in many highly competitive markets and has remained extremely entrepreneurial. Some of its divisions actually meet the target of earning 25 percent of their sales revenues on products developed within the last three years, and its research staff does not have to account for up to 25 percent of its time and can spend it experimenting in any activity that interests it.

To stimulate the entrepreneurial environment, some corporations have spun off subsidiaries. Control Data Corporation (CDC) recently established its own supercomputer division as ETA Systems, Inc., retaining only 40 percent ownership. CDC believed that ETA could respond faster and more flexibly to Japanese competition.[20] Those industries that remain entrepreneurial are those that are highly competitive.

IMPLICATIONS FOR STATE DEVELOPMENT POLICY

> The state cannot by itself create this entrepreneurial spirit—but it can create the conditions that allow it to flourish. It can do this by removing the barriers that currently inhibit growth and development.
>
> Governor Hugh L. Carey, New York, 1981

Entrepreneurs exist in all communities, but the vigor with which they emerge depends upon the entrepreneurial environment—the availability of role models, access to financial institutions, rewards to risk-taking, and above all the absence of barriers.

A development strategy encouraging entrepreneurship offers three advantages:

- It encourages diversification, so that local economies do not become dependent on a single firm or industry.
- Existing state residents are not forced to bear the direct and indirect costs of subsidies to recruit or retain industry from outside the state.
- Entrepreneurs and their backers, and not the community at large, bear the risk of failure.

The most important lesson for state economic policy is that review and reform of economic regulations has an important place in the state's development strategy. In pursuing economic and social goals, federal, state, and local governments have erected barriers to entrepreneurship—laws and regulations that limit entry into occupations and businesses and that limit the ability of businesses to compete.

Changes in the structure of the economy and experimentation by different governments present opportunities for lowering barriers to entrepreneurship. These opportunities can be exploited without sacrificing other public policy objectives. However, creating and maintaining an attractive entrepreneurial climate will require imagination, hard work, and constant vigilance. There will be continued political pressure from different groups to introduce legislation to preserve jobs, keep plants open, restrict competition, protect the consumer, and maintain the quality of life. These issues are critical and should be addressed without unduly dampening the entrepreneurial climate.

A strategy to improve the entrepreneurial climate could have two elements: reducing barriers to entry and establishing a stable fiscal environment.

Removing Barriers to Entrepreneurship.

In recent years, federal, state, and city governments have turned more decisionmaking over to entrepreneurs by deregulating railroads, trucking, airlines, telecommunications, and other industries. Some states have experimented with increased competition in health-care and with competitive bidding for prison management. Many more opportunities exist in the areas of occupational licensing, trade restrictions, agriculture, and financial institutions (Chapter 5). The basic objectives of public policy can in many instances be achieved with less adverse economic impact than current practices impose.

Some elements of a strategy to promote the entrepreneurial environment include:[21]

1. Limit the power of local governments to grant monopolies to cable TV companies and require the phasing out of existing monopolies over time.
2. Eliminate the power of local governments to grant monopolies to cab companies or to limit the number of cabs.[22]
3. Encourage agricultural entrepreneurship. Without abolishing all price and quality controls, it is possible to provide marginal incentives to farmers to innovate in crops and methods.
4. Review state occupational licensing to identify opportunities for divesting state responsibilities to private boards or for eliminating all requirements.
5. Identify regulatory barriers to the provision of services such as health care and day care. Establish carefully monitored demonstration projects to determine the effects of relaxing or reforming regulations.
6. Establish a "one-stop" permitting and assistance program for new enterprises that ensures that these businesses comply with environmental, health, and other regulations with the minimum of effort.
7. Set up a program to review and streamline state regulations with a target of reducing paperwork by 10 percent a year.

Creating a Stable Fiscal Environment.

The state's perennial fiscal goal is to offer its chosen array of public services at the lowest possible cost to residents and businesses. Public facilities and educational programs should not be neglected in order to keep taxes low to attract industry. Such practices usually necessitate a hurried tax increase in the future, which more than compensates for temporary abatements today. States should resist creating additional loopholes to favor preferred industries or localities because these do little more than scatter windfall benefits to selected enterprises and increase the taxes that others must pay.

Fiscal stability also requires longer-term budgeting than most states currently undertake. A revenue surplus one year does not mean that taxes can be cut if the surplus is occurring at the peak of an economic expansion. Such bonuses to voters will have to be retracted when the economy slows. A few states have experimented with stabilization funds that accumulate during periods of rapid economic expansion and augment general revenues during slower periods.[23] The added fiscal stability is a major contribution to the investment climate.

Other policies that can contribute to a stable fiscal environment include:

1. Reduce the rates of personal and business taxes by reducing or eliminating loopholes that favor specific sectors and activities.
2. Eliminate discretionary tax abatement and exemption programs used to attract or retain industry; almost all of these programs create a rapidly growing tax expenditure that constrains the state's ability to lower overall rates or finance needed public services.
3. Select taxes that grow as the need for public services grows—severance taxes, for example, do not grow—and establish long-term growth targets for revenues and expenditures.
4. Employ user fees to finance public services and infrastructure programs wherever administratively and politically feasible.

NOTES

1. Calonius, 1984.

2. See footnote 7, chapter 2.

3. John Diebold has observed (1984, p.35): "In neither Japan nor Germany would it be easy for someone to leave a large company, find venture capital to start a new business, fail in that business, and find it possible either to rejoin his former employer or to enter another large company without an almost ineradicable blot on his record."

4. Traditional economic theory defines competition in terms of the number of businesses in an industry, not the freedom of entry into that industry. The cab industry would meet this definition, but the fact that people are prepared to pay a large amount to enter the industry shows that fares have reached a level only possible when entry is restricted. The air freight business is dominated by four or five firms—too few to satisfy the traditional definition of competition—but entry is not limited, and the industry is highly competitive.

5. Williams, 1982. Those familiar only with Manhattan may believe that New York is relatively well served. Service in the outer boroughs is almost nonexistent.

6. See Sobieski, 1985

7. Traditional economic theory has accorded considerable space to discussing how the conditions of perfect competition can be violated by:
   1) Cartels to Restrict Trade. Existing firms may insulate themselves from further competition by fixing prices, dividing up markets, or restricting entry. Although this is illegal, Adam Smith observed (1776, Bk 1, p.223): "People of the same trade seldom meet together, even for merriment and diversion, but the conversation ends in a conspiracy against the public, or in some contrivance to raise prices." Sometimes the conspirators are aided by natural factors such as technological advances (as IBM has enjoyed at times) and at other times through threat or financial arrangements. Cartels are vigorously prosecuted by the Justice Department. But even before federal oversight, most cartels had unstable and short-lived because any one member could gain on others by breaking the agreement, cutting prices, and capturing a larger share of the market.
   2) Economies of scale. The four U.S. automobile makers have enjoyed freedom from domestic competition by enormous economies of scale, yielding a cost advantage that virtually precludes any additional domestic makers (except for specialty cars). The commercial airframe industry also enjoys such enormous economies of scale that only one domestic firm may survive (Newhouse, 1982). However, economies of scale are less important from the perspective of world markets. Auto imports have introduced a strong, and resented, element of competition. Also the **potential** of another firm or firms entering an industry may be more than enough to ensure that existing firms behave competitively. Where there are economies of scale, the new entrant is typically not a new firm but a large existing company that is moving into the industry. Economies of scale are more important in theory than in practice.

8. See Craig and Sailors, 1984 and Williams, 1982.

9. The failures of savings institutions in Ohio in the spring of 1985 illustrate the reasons for this concern. Although some people have interpreted the crisis as evidence of the need for increased regulation and greater restrictions on entry and investment practices, the problem is one of inappropriate rather than inadequate regulation.

10. See Danzon in Moore, 1984.

11. In some cities this includes laws prohibiting the erection of dish antenna, since these are direct rivals.

12. While there is a natural monopoly for laying the cable network, there is no monopoly on the programming the network can carry, since most systems carry many channels. Early systems may have carried a dozen channels, but current fiber optic systems may carry more than 100 channels. Cities could separate the franchise process into a cable laying contract and then auction access to the channels. A decision by the Ninth U.S. Circuit Court of Appeals in the spring of 1985 may end the practice of granting monopolies. In the case of Preferred Communications Inc. vs. the City of Los Angeles, the court found that a communications company that challenged Los Angeles' monopoly franchise was protected by the first amendment.

13. Craig and Sailors, 1984.

14. A dramatic illustration is provided by Alicia Paige, a black woman from Avon, Massachusetts (quoted from **INC,** July 1985, p.49):

> Everything collapsed for me in one year, 1978. My sister died in October, my divorce became final in November, and I had to sell my home in December. So, at that point, what do you do? There I stand, a woman 57 years old—where do I go from there?
>
> When I was in Randolph Library, we used to have what they called the interlibrary loan service; sometimes it would take six months to get the book that you wanted yesterday. So I said, now, wouldn't it be interesting if I could put all of the South Shore library holdings on one database, and put a CRT in each library, and make the librarians feel like they're big computer operators? They could call up a book by author, title or subject, and they would know immediately where the book was and what library it was in.
>
> I talked with my brothers, and they said, Well, go ahead and try. I said, Yeah, but suppose the business fails? What am I going to do? Where am I going to live? My brothers said, You've always got us, you can come and live with us until you get back on your feet.
>
> I sold my house for the start-up money, and I knew that it was all I had. If the business did not prosper and bring in money, then I would eventually have to go bankrupt. I used to wake up in the middle of the night—you know, I'd be sound asleep—and all of a sudden, I'd wake up, and I'd sit straight up in bed, and say, Am I crazy?
>
> I never thought of just a small business. I said, no, if I'm going to start a business, I might as well go big. Like IBM. I'd like to keep going so I can say I have $1 billion in orders. I would love to say that! I don't ever expect to, but I'm looking that way. I never thought that we would do close to $6 million in business. But we did.

15. U.S. Government Accounting Office, 1981.

16. Freeman, 1971 and Gellman, 1976.

17. Gellman, 1976.

18. See Peters and Waterman, 1982.

19. **Wall Street Journal,** January 6, 1984, p.22.

20. **Business Week,** October 17, 1983, p.159.

21. Those policies dealing with financial institutions are discussed in Chapter 5.

22. This may be required as a result of U.S. Justice Department action against the State of Minnesota that successfully challenged the State's power to allow local monopolies.

23. Michigan created a well-designed fund into which payments are made automatically depending on the growth rate of personal income. It is described in detail in Vaughan, 1980.

PART 2: INVESTMENT

INVESTING IN INNOVATION

Business? That's very simple: it's other people's money.
Alexander Dumas (1857)

Few people are rich enough to finance their entrepreneurial ventures from their own resources and most firms do not have enough retained earnings to finance all the projects they believe are worthwhile. They must turn to those with money to invest. The capital market brings investors together with entrepreneurs. Our capacity to translate innovative ideas into new productive capacity depends not only on how much is invested but on how well the capital market performs its function of channeling investors' funds toward the most promising investments. Effective financial institutions are a vitally important part of a healthy entrepreneurial environment.

This chapter examines how well financial institutions are meeting demands for business investment and identifies the role for state and local governments in the process. The widespread belief that there are "gaps" in the capital market has led states to create development finance programs to provide loans or loan guarantees to small and minority-owned businesses. Recently many states, concerned that they are not getting their share of venture capital placements, have established publicly chartered corporations to direct investments or tax credits to encourage private investments. Yet these efforts have rarely proceeded from a careful analysis of how the capital market operates or of how state actions, including regulatory and tax policy, influence the behavior of financial institutions. This chapter analyzes these issues.

The first section examines the overall pattern of investment in the United States because this sets the context within which state policies operate: Is there enough saving? How is the pattern of investment distorted by taxes and regulations? The second section briefly describes the roles played by financial institutions in allocating capital and discusses perceptions about how well capital markets bring together those with capital and those who need it. The final two sections focus specifically on the requirements of small and new enterprises, analyzing whether gaps exist in the availability of equity and debt capital for entrepreneurial ventures and how state policies influence those parts of the capital market.

DO WE INVEST ENOUGH AND WISELY?

When the national economy appeared to weaken during the 1970s, the inadequacy and ineffectiveness of business investment were frequently diagnosed as causes. While there is little evidence that inadequate savings have constrained the rate of investment in the past (although tax disincentives to saving may become important in the future), there is evidence that the tax code and regulatory policies distort investments in a way that penalizes new businesses through favoring investments by older established firms.

Do We Save Enough?

In the long-run, the economy can invest no more than it saves. A sacrifice of current consumption is necessary to finance all types of investment. Savings by businesses (retained profits and depreciation allowances) and by households have averaged about 17 percent of GNP in recent years. The tax code penalizes saving through the double taxation of dividend income (corporate income is taxed and then distributed dividends are taxed again), the deductibility of consumer debt interest, and the double taxation of savings income (offset somewhat by the creation of IRAs). However, the savings rate appears not to have increased in response to dramatic reductions in the tax rates on savings income. (Savings are, however, one of the most difficult economic variables to measure accurately.)[1]

There is ample theoretical and empirical evidence that federal and most state tax codes tax the income from capital more heavily than the income from labor, leading to an "inefficiently low" rate of investment.[2] There is also evidence that the high and fluctuating inflation rates prevailing during much of the last decade raised the effective tax rates on capital investments and therefore reduced the rate of capital formation.[3]

There is very little evidence to support the view that inadequate savings constrained growth in the late 1970s. While the rate of investment was falling, real interest rates were also falling. By the late 1970s, market interest rates were at record levels, but real interest rates were much lower than they had been during the expansionary 1960s.[4] Thus the more serious problem during this inflationary period was not the lack of funds to finance investment but the low rate of return after taxes on productive investments relative to other income earning assets such as real estate and tax shelters.

How Well Do We Invest?

Several economists have alleged that the structure rather than the level of taxes has slowed economic growth.[5] For any given overall rate of investment, economic growth will proceed more slowly if investments are not directed toward the most productive opportunities. The relative rates of return expected on alternative investment opportunities determine how capital is allocated, and these rates of return are shaped by the preferential tax treatment accorded to certain types of investment. Tax preferences, including investment tax credits, accelerated depreciation, capital gains exclusions,[6] and excess oil depletion allowances, create tax expenditures that are a multiple of the volume of revenues generated by the corporate income tax.[7] Most major federal tax preferences are mirrored in state tax codes. States add loopholes of their own to support established local industries, such as worm farming in Virginia and horse breeding in Kentucky to vineyards in New York and oil refining in Louisiana.

Tax preferences have three effects on capital markets: first, by reducing rates they increase the overall level of investment; second, they shift capital from less favored to more favored types of investment, which reduces the efficiency of investment; and third, they increase federal and state borrowing or increase other taxes, which deters development.

From the point of view of an entrepreneur, the most important distortions are: federal credit policies that support established industries; business tax bias toward physical capital;[8] homeownership subsidies;[9] double taxation of dividend income;[10] and tax provisions encouraging takeovers and mergers.[11]

FINANCIAL CAPITAL MARKETS:[12]

At any given time, there are many different parties trying to finance new ventures—from people wishing to open restaurants and engineers trying to develop new prototypes to governments wanting to finance new roads and large corporations planning to open new branches. There are also many sources of funds, from retained earnings of businesses and pension funds of employees to government surpluses and household savings. Projects differ in their size and risk and in the types and sources of information needed to evaluate them. Investors differ in their willingness to bear risk, their knowledge of investment opportunities, and their wealth.

Investors and Institutions

To accommodate the various demands of these participants, many different mechanisms have evolved for matching investors with entrepreneurs. There are informal "markets" of family members and friends who are investors in more than nine out of ten new enterprises. People close to the entrepreneur have much better information on his or her talents and creditworthiness than could be acquired by any banker or venture capitalist. Those requiring more capital and possessing some evidence of the technical and commercial feasibility of their idea may turn to a venture capitalist—a partnership or corporation of investors who are prepared to offer capital and management expertise in return for a share of the possible rewards.[13] Other projects that involve much less risk may be able to use unsecured bank credit, or, in the case of entrepreneurs within a large corporation, innovation may be financed from retained earnings or from the sale of corporate equity or debt.

Savers and investors usually act through financial intermediaries such as commercial banks, insurance companies, and brokers. These intermediaries reduce the costs of search, analysis, acquisition, and diversification of investments, providing a higher rate of return to savers and lower costs to investors.[14] State and federal regulations restrict the scope of financial intermediation. For example, commercial banks are not allowed to take an equity position in companies to which they lend. This restriction and the cost of acquiring information have led different institutions to specialize in serving different savers and investors. A brief classification of the main financial intermediaries includes:

- **Commercial banks** raise their funds from consumers and by borrowing; they specialize in making short- to medium-term business loans and consumer finance, and have extensive branch networks.
- **Venture capital corporations** raise their funds from institutional investors (pension funds, etc.) and from wealthy people; they specialize in financing larger new enterprises and new technology ventures.
- **Insurance companies** raise most of their funds from individuals and provide long-term debt to large-scale commercial and industrial projects.
- **Investment banks** are often capitalized as partnerships and act as intermediaries selling corporate and municipal debt to institutional investors.

These institutions try to place savers' money in the most profitable investments compatible with the savers' willingness to take risks and time preference.

Performance of Capital Markets

The availability of funding for viable business projects is crucial to the development process. How well the capital market performs its task is hotly debated.[15] On the one hand, some observers are inclined to believe bankers when they claim to be financing every viable project. They thus conclude that capital markets work perfectly.[16] They fail to realize that bankers are operating within a regulatory and tax environment (as well as within an institutional framework) that limits the definition of what bankers mean by "viable."

At the other extreme, some critics of capital markets listen to the complaints of would-be entrepreneurs who have been denied credit. They regard the importance of informal sources of capital to new businesses as evidence of capital market "gaps."[17] These views are often used to justify the creation of public capital agencies or the imposition of regulations on investors and lenders.

But the evidence can be deceiving. The fact that some entrepreneurs, initially refused capital, later go on to triumph, or that small business pays higher interest rates on its loans is not evidence of "market failure." Investment decisions are made on **expected** rates of return, and foresight is always less reliable than hindsight. Many projects are so risky that a conventional lender or investor cannot justify committing funds to them. A hypothetical portfolio of these high-risk projects would include some that are eventually successful, but overall the portfolio would be a losing proposition. It would be no more profitable if it were owned by a public agency than a private institution.

The bulk of the evidence leads to the rejection of extreme views. Capital markets, for the most part, work fairly well in sorting out the millions of potential investments that reward investors for risks taken. But the tax and regulatory environment discourages risk-taking by financial institutions, and the high cost of information can make it difficult for small and new ventures to secure backing, as will be seen below.

These conclusions do not support claims for public intervention in capital markets in the form of requirements for more small business lending or the creation of a public agency to finance projects that cannot get funding under the current system. The cost of the intervention may well exceed any benefits it bestows. A public lending agency may operate at a loss and further discourage private banks from becoming more entrepreneurial in their lending. It may be more efficient to change the regulatory and tax measures that discourage risk-taking.

From the perspective of entrepreneurship, two aspects of the capital market are of special importance: the availability of equity capital for start-ups and expansions of young companies and the availability of short- and medium-term bank credit. Determining whether there is a shortage of either type of capital has been the focus of many studies and programs. To increase the availability or lower the cost of these capital components has been the target of many federal, state, or local programs.

EQUITY CAPITAL

Equity capital—claims of ownership and participation in the profits of an enterprise—is particularly important for new enterprises or for existing businesses undergoing a major expansion or introduction of new products. Few new enterprises could afford the debt-service payments if all their capital were raised through borrowing. Equity capital does not require firms to make regular repayments, and investors receive no steady income stream. They must wait upon the success of the enterprise to earn a return.

A business enterprise requires equity at different stages and will turn to different types of investors at different stages. As economist Lawrence Litvak observes (1982, p.3):

> A business enterprise must be able to tap different sources and kinds of capital at different times over its life cycle. Foreclosing any one source can have the same effect as depriving a developing organism of a vital nutrient.

During the last five years, venture capital—equity capital for fledgling enterprises from formal sources (involved in 0.25 percent of all startups)—has captured the attention of policy-makers because it has been available in very limited amounts and only in a few states. Concern arose in the mid-1970s when the rate of new venture placements declined and the new issues market collapsed.[18] With the disappearance of new venture funds, only the most promising new businesses were funded. The causes of this were:

- *The capital gains tax increase* in 1971 to a maximum rate of 70 percent (venture investors earn most of their return in the form of capital gains);

- The passage of the *Employees Retirement Income Security Act* (ERISA) in 1974 that drove pension funds away from the venture market because of its ambivalent definition of the prudent investor rule;
- *Inflation* diverted some of the savings of those willing to take risks into real estate projects;
- Finally, in reaction to the collapse of hundreds of new issues in the stock market slump of 1969, the *Securities and Exchange Commission* (SEC) tightened up the rules governing new issues—by 1976 the costs of issues of less than $5 million were 10 percent of funds raised, compared to less than 2 percent of funds raised for issues of more than $100 million.

The results were dramatic. The volume of new stock issues—one of the best measures of entrepreneurial activity—fell from $1.3 billion in 1969 to $16 million in 1975:

Each of these problems has been resolved:

- The capital gains tax rate was reduced in 1978 and again in 1981. In addition, generous research and development tax credits were enacted in 1981, spawning hundreds of R and D partnerships investing in new enterprises and in new products.
- ERISA guidelines were finally clarified in 1979, and pensions now provide between one-third and one-half of the new venture funds each year.
- The inflation rate has fallen from 20 percent to 4 percent.[19]
- The SEC has streamlined filing procedures for small new issues.

The recovery has been striking. The dollar volume of new issues in 1983 approached the 1969 level in real terms. New private capital committed to venture capital firms increased from $39 million in 1977 to more than $2 billion in 1983. However, the recovery of the venture industry has thus far been concentrated in a few high-tech industries in California, Massachusetts, New York, and Texas. This concentration is declining.

The rebound in formal venture placements has been accompanied by a boom in over-the-counter stock issues—stock issued on local stock exchanges and not traded nationally. States vary greatly with respect to the way they regulate local issues. Some require even more detailed disclosure than the SEC, which makes the cost of a small issue prohibitive. Other states take a caveat emptor approach to these issues, which greatly reduces the cost of the issue and increases the risk to the investor. Securities regulation reform may be an important part of a state's development strategy.

Formal venture capital corporations were involved in only 1500 out of 600,000 startups in 1984. These were mostly larger firms based upon new technologies. Most entrepreneurs had to rely on their own financial resources, those of family and friends, or local bank loans. This makes the ability to start a business dependent on the income of an entrepreneur and not just upon the viability of the business plan. It is difficult, however, to overcome this handicap, because a centralized public agency cannot acquire the information needed to evaluate potential entrepreneurs. In addition, public agencies are subject to political pressures on their selection of projects which may lead them to pick projects that are not the best risks.

The focus on venture capital has diverted attention away from other aspects of the equity capital problem that can be addressed more effectively through public policy. The personal tax code discourages risk-taking by individual investors. For example, although capital losses can be offset against capital gains when computing taxable income, they can only be offset against personal income up to $3,000 in any one year. The rest of the loss must be carried forward. All gains are subject to immediate taxation. In addition, the progressive structure of the personal income tax discourages risk-taking (McCaleb, 1982, p.3):

> The present tax system limits the liability for losses incurred on investments. Furthermore, due to the progressive rate structure, the government's share in the losses is less than the government's share in gains. For these reasons, the existing tax system tends to discourage risk-taking as compared to a proportional tax rate with complete loss allowances.

The bias against risk-taking built into the tax structure is reinforced by the way financial institutions are regulated. Commercial banks would be the logical source of small equity investments because they have, or can acquire at relatively low cost, detailed information about the past business performance and personal creditworthiness of the entrepreneur. Yet they are precluded from taking an equity position by the Glass-Steagall Act. A "near equity" alternative—loans with an equity kicker[20] attached—is permitted under a ruling by the Comptroller of the Currency but is rarely used because of uncertain tax treatment and, in many states, the potential of violating usury ceilings. Many public pension funds, which control more than $300 billion in assets, are prohibited from making equity investments in new enterprises by state regulations. Private insurance companies also face restrictions, imposed by state regulators, on the types of investments they may include in their portfolios.

In summary, although the availability of formal venture capital has greatly increased recently, entrepreneurs in many parts of the country and in many industries still face a shortage of equity as a result of shortsighted federal and state policies. Market pressures will eventually fill these "gaps," but we cannot predict how rapidly. However, the issue of formal venture capital is much less important than that of encouraging equity capital through less formal channels, since the latter are used in almost all startups.

DEBT CAPITAL

It is widely believed by public officials and economists that new and small businesses face special problems in securing debt capital for both long-term investments in plant and equipment and short-term inventory finance. This belief is reflected in the formation of the Small Business Administration, the passage of the Community Reinvestment Act of 1978, and in the loan guarantee programs offered by almost all states and by hundreds of cities and counties.

There is, however, no reliable evidence of large "gaps" in capital availability either for all enterprises or for small and minority owned businesses that have traditionally been the target of state development efforts. There is reason to believe, however, that the current tax and regulatory policies employed by state and federal governments do discourage risk-taking by banks. This creates difficulties for new and small businesses and for businesses in neighborhoods or industries that are perceived as "risky."

Small Business Lending

Much of the apparent bias against small and new businesses is a rational response to the greater risk in lending to small businesses and the higher costs of assembling and processing the data needed to make a loan decision.[21] "Operating costs" per dollar of loan are much higher for small loans than for large loans, and the differential in operating costs per dollar exceeds the differential in interest rates earned on the loans.[22] In other words, although banks charge small borrowers a higher rate, this premium does not fully compensate for the higher costs.

There are two reasons why banks may subsidize lending to new enterprises: first, to establish a relationship with an enterprise that may grow to be a larger borrower in the future; and second, to establish a connection with entrepreneurs in the hope of selling them more profitable services such as consumer credit, investment services, or payroll processing. Lending to new borrowers is, therefore, a loss leader.

Some banks may be able to profitably expand their small and new business lending because their internal accounting procedures lead them to underestimate the value of the business generated. Most large banks are organized around centralized "profit centers" that must achieve growth, revenue, and profit targets. In many banks, small-business lending units are separated from consumer lending, investment management, corporate banking, and other services. Because there is rarely a mechanism for sharing the profits among profit centers, small-business lending does not appear to perform well even if it is successfully bringing in new customers to the other banking units. These market gaps are more likely to be filled by banks if there are few barriers to entry in the banking markets.

The pressure to centralize and compartmentalize has arisen from the desire to cut the costs of handling information, to enjoy the benefits of specialization, and to establish direct accountability. Smaller banks, or banks that allow greater discretion at the branch level, appear to be more aware of the advantages of small-business lending. The difference in approach is illustrated in the following account of the practices of the Chase Manhattan Bank and the Chemical Bank in New York City:

> Carl Gustavson, senior vice president in charge of Chase Manhattan's community bank division, said that last year the bank had set up a special unit to deal with loan applications from small businesses. The applications are gathered at branches and sent to the special unit for approval.
>
> 'We recognize that small companies don't have the same kind of financial statements that big corporations do, and that's why we set up the special unit to concentrate our expertise,' Mr. Gustavson said. But by moving the loan application-approval process beyond the branches, it also separates the function from the businessman. Those banks that have efficiently geared up their small business activities are enthusiastic about the field because, done properly, it can be more lucrative than lending to bigger companies with more bargaining power.
>
> More than most banks, Chemical seems to have adjusted to the needs of small business.
>
> 'It all depends on personal relationships at the branch level,' said [Chemical Bank senior vice president, Walter] Lipp. 'Its a very personal business.'
>
> Unlike most other large banks, Chemical's branch managers have the authority to make loans of up to $100,000, and they are paid bonuses for generating such business.[23]

In New York City the competition among major financial institutions is sufficiently intense that one bank explored the market for lending to new and small business. In smaller states the competition may not be as fierce and may be further repressed by anticompetitive regulations that limit branch banking, prevent out-of-state banks from doing business in state, or limit the activities of non-bank institutions. States must use their regulatory policies to encourage competition among the state's financial institutions to improve the climate for small business lending.

This example also illustrates the difficulty confronting a state or local government agency established to lend to small businesses. It cannot possibly duplicate the branch network and loan officer expertise that Chemical Bank found was essential for its effort. A state agency may, if it is successful, assemble a portfolio of 30 loans, serving a tiny fraction of the state's small business community. It is likely to suffer from a high default rate because the state has poorer information than private lenders. A policy to encourage increased risk-taking by commercial banks would improve capital access to the entire business community and would not impose such direct costs on the taxpayer.

Regulations and Risk-Taking

State and federal regulations discourage risk-taking by lenders. Comparison of banks' behavior under different regulatory structures indicates that greater competition in the banking system is likely to make more capital available to smaller businesses.[24]

In states where branch banking is allowed, the competition in banking makes credit more readily available to smaller businesses at slightly lower interest rates. Because large firms borrow in national rather than local capital markets, their borrowing is not affected by state restrictions on banking structure.

Branch banks rely less heavily on relatively expensive "purchased money" than unit banks and have more stable deposits and thus lower-cost funds.[25] The often-expressed fear that large, multi-branch banks would tend to focus on large corporate customers[26] ignores the fact that large banks have much higher loan-to-asset ratios than small banks[27]—that is, they invest a smaller share of their assets in securities and therefore can meet the loan demands of both small and large customers.[28] A detailed study of bank lending data revealed that: "Statewide branching has resulted in a greater proportion of business loans to locally-limited businesses (small, local firms) than either unit banking or limited branching."[29]

In a few instances branch banking has led to increased concentration—in small states and in sparsely populated rural areas—and a higher cost of credit to small borrowers.[30] In larger, less concentrated markets, banks tend to specialize in certain types of lending or in lending to certain industries, which allows them to meet the special needs of entrepreneurs.[31]

In addition to banking structure, other aspects of bank regulation influence banks' lending policies. For example, loan classification procedures deter risk-taking.[32] The Comptroller of the Currency classifies loans if the borrower is highly leveraged, has no long-term experience, or fails to meet other criteria.[33] Classification of a loan requires the lender to increase reserves, and, what is even more costly, to file biweekly reports. Loan officers can oversee only half as many classified loans as regular loans. The Comptroller's regulations do not allow banks to set up special "high-risk loan pools" (although special permission may be given). The excessive focus on default rate may be misplaced—a bank with a default rate in excess of one percent is not necessarily doing badly if it is earning 5 percentage points over its cost of money, compared with a bank with a 0.5 percent loss rate that is earning only 3 percent above its money cost. State bank regulators could encourage lending to higher-risk enterprises by encouraging the development of a secondary market in small loans.

Risk-taking is also deterred by state usury laws that prevent banks from making "equity kicker" loans—loans in which the bank takes a share of gross sales, net income, or some other performance-related income in lieu of some or all of the regular interest payments. These are allowed under a ruling by the Comptroller of the Currency and would be the ideal way of financing riskier loans because the bank would collect from the winners what it loses on others. However, ambiguity over the status of these payments relative to state usury ceilings and to federal and state taxes has successfully prevented banks from using this tool.[34]

IMPLICATIONS FOR STATE DEVELOPMENT POLICY

The most important policy implication gained from this discussion is that states should review the ways they regulate the finance industry and tax the earnings of investors to develop ways to encourage riskier investments and loans without jeopardizing the integrity of the institutions. The purpose is not to compel banks, other institutions, and even individuals to suffer a lower rate of return and a higher chance of bankruptcy, but to allow them to "price" risk more easily. Pricing risk involves earning a higher rate of return from successful but risky ventures to compensate for a higher default or failure rate on the losers, without encountering tax or regulatory barriers. If capital were shifted from its current safe haven to a hypothetical portfolio of riskier projects, society as a whole would gain a higher yield on its investments.

Second, states should avoid setting up public institutions to stimulate the flow of capital for business investment. Successfully operating a financial institution requires a high level of expertise, detailed local information, and a diversified portfolio—characteristics that public agencies have difficulty in attaining; they can rarely pay salaries high enough to retain the best personnel; they are not part of an extensive network; and they are too small to diversify effectively. On top of these problems, they face the political necessity of showing quick results and the pressure to assist enterprises associated with elected officials. Because of these pressures, few state or local lending or equity investing agencies have proved successful. Many are very conservative and are merely displacing private investments. Others, especially those targeted at minority businesses, have loss rates in excess of 30 percent.

Third, states should encourage competition among financial institutions whenever possible. Protected industries—such as banks in unit-banking states—are less aggressive in their lending.

Finally, while there are examples of successful public finance agencies, states "play the percentages" and recognize that the chances of success and the rewards for success are also slight. A successful public development agency can serve a minute number of firms. This will have much less impact than a regulatory reform or tax change that induced each bank in the state to make one loan it would not have made before.

A successful agency may demonstrate to the local banking community that certain types of risk can be absorbed (just as the Federal Housing Administration demonstrated that 20 year mortgages were "bankable"). But it is unlikely that the agency will greatly improve the entrepreneurial climate.

Therefore, states should consider the following initiatives:

- Repeal of usury ceilings or an amendment to exclude bank lending or equity kicker payments from the ceiling;
- Reform of state capital gains taxes to treat gains on "collectibles" (such as gold and antiques) as ordinary income; for example, California and New York abolished the capital gains enjoyed on investments in new businesses, and California raised the rate on collectibles;

- Ensure that Subchapter S corporations enjoy the same exemption from corporate income tax under state law that they enjoy under federal law; this is a common organizational form for venture capital corporations;
- Permit state-chartered banks (and savings and loans) to establish "entrepreneurial" portfolios (that cannot exceed one or two percent of net worth) of riskier loans to new and young enterprises that will not be classified but judged on their overall performance;
- Encourage the development of private insurance of commercial and industrial loans; in many states insurance companies are precluded from insuring such loans although experience with the insurance of municipal loans suggests that this can improve market access to riskier borrowers;
- Set up security regulations that allow for the easy issue of new small issues;
- Expand the capacity of commercial banks to compete by removing any restrictions on branching within the state and allow out-of-state banks to enter the market;
- Review restrictive legal lists that restrict investments by public pension funds, trusts, and state-chartered institutions more narrowly than is allowed under the "prudent investor" rule.

NOTES

1. See "The Deepening Mystery of the Savings Rate," **Business Week,** August 6, 1984, p.68. Gross savings excludes individual capital gains. The large cuts in federal personal and corporate income tax rates in 1981 were predicated on the belief that the national economy was being held back through lack of savings. Some argued that, because the United States had a rate of personal savings (around 6 or 7 percent) that was less than half the rate prevailing in other developed countries, interest rates had been driven up and investment discouraged. The theme of inadequate savings is discussed by Lester Thurow (1980), Ira Magaziner and Robert Reich (1982), Robert Reich (1984), and Felix Rohatyn (1984).

2. Feldstein, 1980.

3. See Henderson in Johnson, 1984.

4. Feldstein, 1982.

5. See Henderson, in Johnson (1984), Thurow (1981), Magaziner and Reich (1981). The weaknesses of the current tax system have also been widely debated as a result of the release of successive plans for tax reform by the U. S. Treasury in 1984 and 1985.

6. A neutral treatment of capital gains would be to exclude from taxation that part of the gain attributable to inflation and tax the rest as normal income. The exclusion of 60 percent of capital gains from taxation, as the present system does,

is an arbitrary approach that creates windfall gains or losses depending upon the rate of inflation.

7. In 1984, the U.S. budget showed tax expenditures in excess of $300 billion, compared with direct expenditures of $800 billion in corporate income tax receipts of about $40 billion. The popular argument that tax expenditures do not count because they presume that all income is taxable has more rhetorical appeal than analytic usefulness. A tax credit that returns $100 million dollars to corporate taxpayers in return for certain investments is identical to the same tax without the credit and a grant program that handed out $100 million to corporations undertaking certain types of investments.

8. Overall, the tax code favors investments in physical capital, which benefits many declining industries relative to investments in human capital. Writing in 1981, three observers (Botkin, Dimancescu, and Stata, 1982, p.3) noted:

> [National economic] policy, embedded in the new tax laws provides accelerated depreciation of capital investments, liberalized investment tax credits . . . On the face of it, incentives for capital investment seem like a good economic idea, and in some respects they are. But . . . this policy reinforces capital-intensive "sunset" industries at the expense of knowledge intensive "sunrise" industries. Even worse, this policy prolongs the lives of dying companies and ignores the needs of growing industries.

9. The combination of high inflation and the favorable tax treatment of home ownership during the 1970s led to a massive increase in investment in residential property at the expense of investments in plant, equipment, and investment in new business (Cagan, 1977)

10. Dividends are taxed twice—first through the corporate income tax and then through the personal income tax. This encourages corporations to retain rather than to distribute income and to be content to earn a relatively lower rate of return on internal investments than they would if they were borrowing the money (McClure, 1979). A very large fraction of retained earnings is concentrated in a few large corporations. By 1979, 50 percent of the nation's savings were in the form of retained earnings and depreciation allowances (**Survey of Current Business,** March 1980). Because of the corporate income tax structure, established businesses enjoy a cheaper source of capital than those that must borrow or attract outside investors.

11. Many argue that these retained earnings encourage "paper entrepreneurship"— paper shuffling (mergers, acquisitions, and divestitures) that provide artificial financial gains without increasing the productive capacity of the economy. There have been a few well-publized examples of fruitless merger activity that have seemed imprudent, the most striking of which was Bendix' ill-fated attempt to acquire Martin-Marrietta.

    However, the threat of a takeover is a strong incentive for good management. If a corporation has low expected earnings, its stock price will be depressed to a level where the company becomes an attractive investment to those who believe that they can manage it more profitably. Examination of the effects of mergers on corporate earnings shows that most takeovers increase the earnings of both the acquiring and the acquired company and are followed by cost-cutting measures (Weston, 1980). States influence the takeover process through securities regulations. In recent years, several states have acted to make takeovers more difficult, and evidence suggests this has doubled the price they must pay for the stock of target firms. By reducing the threat of takeover, the competitive environment is impaired, which may reduce the economy's competitiveness in the long-run.

12. For a brief introduction see Litvak and Daniels, 1979 and Hansen, 1981.

13. Venture capitalists are involved in less than one quarter of one percent of start-ups. Ben and Jerry are much more typical. To start their ice cream business, they used $6,000 of their own savings, a $2,000 loan from Jerry's father, and $4,000 from a Burlington, Vermont, bank. Most venture capitalists do not like to provide seed capital. As one venture capitalist observed: "If someone comes to me and says he needs $300,000 in seed money, he's not an entrepreneur." (See **Illinois Issues,** October, 1984, p.26)

14. Solomon and Pringle, 1980, p.34ff.

15. For a discussion of capital market failure, see Litvak and Daniels, 1979 and Daniels and Kieschnick, 1978.

16. Unfortunately there have been very few studies of how well capital markets work. In 1939 William O. Douglas, when chairman of the Securities and Exchange Commission, lamented the lack of research that would allow us to better understand capital. Little has been done since then to fill the gap. Three techniques have been employed to address the question of how well capital markets perform: surveys of existing firms, examinations of the behavior of financing institutions, and theoretical analyses of the operations of capital markets. All of these methods have weaknesses.

    Surveys of businesses are usually based on such questions as: "Have you ever been refused credit by a commercial lender?" or "Have you ever experienced difficulty in securing investment capital on favorable terms?" The survey population inevitably excludes those new businesses that were never born or existing businesses that were forced to close because they could not get credit. And "experiencing difficulty" does not indicate a capital market gap if it reflected poor management by the entrepreneur.

    Surveys of financing institutions have the opposite bias. Venture capitalists lament the lack of good deals when competition in the industry compels them to seek harder for a good project. Commercial banks blame entrepreneurs for an inadequate track record, while actually denying credit to conform to regulations.

    Finally, studies that identify theoretical reasons why capital markets do not work efficiently focus on regulation, taxes, risk aversion, and high transactions cost (Litvak and Daniels, 1979). But they can provide no measure of the severity of these problems or the capacity of the market to develop structures and procedures to overcome these barriers. However, they do provide a theoretical framework for starting to analyze capital markets and have yielded some testable hypotheses.

17. For a discussion of capital gaps see New England Capital Commission, 1976 and Council for Northeast Economic Action, 1981.

18. The collapse of the new issues market meant that venture capitalists were unable to liquidate their investments in new enterprises by "taking them public" through issuing publicly traded stock for the first time.

19. Had capital gains been "inflation indexed"—that is, the value of the proceeds from the sale of the asset would be deflated by the increase in the Consumer Price Index (or some other index) since the original purchase of the asset—the sudden and unpredicted inflation would have had no effect.

20. The Comptroller of the Currency has ruled (7.7312):

    A national bank may take as consideration for a loan a share of the profit, income or earnings from a business enterprise of a borrower. Such share may be in addition to or in lieu of interest. The borrower's obligation to repay principal, however, shall not be conditioned upon the profit, income, or earnings of the business enterprise.

This payment in lieu of interest is known as an equity kicker. It would allow banks to establish a "higher risk" portfolio in which they would earn higher rates of return on successful ventures to compensate for a higher risk and therefore a higher default rate (Brophy, 1982).

21. Heggestad and Rhoads, 1978.

22. Murphy, 1982.

23. **New York Times,** May 5, 1982. According to Mr. Lipp, this policy has more than doubled its small business checking account deposits over the past five years, to $1.3 billion from $600 million. 24. However, it is difficult to document this because bank loan data rarely record either the age or the size of the borrower (Savage, 1982).

25. See Rhoads, 1980 and Lausch and Murphy, 1970.

26. See Guttentag and Herman, 1967.

27. See Curry, 1978.

28. See Felsenfeld, 1980.

29. See Eisenbeis, 1975.

30. Heggestad and Rhoads, 1978.

31. Eastburn and Balles, 1958 and Shull, 1982.

32. See Litvak and Daniels, 1980 and Hansen, 1981.

33. "Classification" is a procedure for drawing attention to potentially troublesome loans and ensuring that the lender gives them appropriate attention. It is worth noting that none of the major crisis banks in recent years—from First Pennsylvania to Continental Illinois—got into difficulties because of lending to small and new businesses or because of classified small business loans.

34. Brophy, 1981.

CHAPTER 6

INVESTING IN HUMAN CAPITAL

> A little reflection will show that the rate of capital formation
> to which economists give so much attention is a secondary
> factor.... The basic factor in an economy's development
> must be the rate of 'brain formation'—the rate at which a
> country produces people with imagination and vision,
> education, theoretical and analytical skills.
>
> Peter Drucker (1977, p. 63)

Training has traditionally been part of a state's economic development strategy. Most states provide subsidized training as an inducement to relocating companies. But human capital investments, such
as training, play a much broader role in a state's development than
simply through specially designed training programs. The major
source of growth in all states is the rate of improvement in the
education and skills of the workforce. Development depends on the
rate at which we accumulate **human capital:**[1] "the knowledge and
skills that people accumulate through education, training, and or
experience that enable them to supply valuable productive service to
others."[2] The education attainments of a state's labor force are not
only a determinant of the overall rate of development but will determine the incidence of poverty. The acquisition of marketable human
capital is also the surest way of elevating people's earnings above the
poverty level.

By the end of the century, the one occupation career may be
history. The rapid pace of technological advance, with its unpredictable twists and turns, threatens almost every skill and occupation
with obsolescence. Retraining and reemploying workers will assume
new importance, and the pace of economic development will depend
in large measure on how quickly workforces can be redeployed. Efficient redeployment will require large investments in human capital.
Entrepreneurs also need to acquire the skills required to set up and
manage a new enterprise. Yet at all levels, from first grade to post-
graduate study, our capacity to make these needed investments is
being questioned.

Investing in education and training is not easy for many people.
Such investments are risky and costly.[3] The payoff periods may be
long and delayed, and changes in technology and market conditions

can make the "salvage value" of patiently acquired skills negligible. Obtaining reliable information is in many instances impossible, and finding financial resources difficult.

Not everyone, however, is ready for or would benefit from retraining. Many of those left jobless from the decline of employment in durable goods manufacturing may lack the basic skills needed to hold other jobs or to acquire more marketable skills. For these people, remedial education rather than retraining may be the appropriate measure. Lack of basic education is a major cause of prolonged joblessness and welfare dependency, but few states provide a comprehensive program to ensure that all adults can read and write. A cursory training program or assistance in job hunting, which is all most people receive under public training programs for the poor, cannot overcome the handicap of basic illiteracy.

State governments play a major role in the human capital investment process: they help fund most primary, secondary, and postsecondary education; they administer the Job Service to help fill job vacancies; they regulate many aspects of the workplace, from safety and health to wages and hours; they operate income maintenance programs that influence labor-force participation rates; and their tax structure influences the relative rate of return on different types of human capital investments.

The first section of this chapter examines the special nature of the decision to invest in ourselves and why the state has a role in helping finance human capital investments. The second section describes the important role that state government plays as provider of information—information that is vital to people in choosing what sort of investment to make and where to make it and to administrators for measuring the performance of different institutions. The third section discusses the government's role in financing education and training, distinguishing between financing institutions and financing people. The fourth section explores the effect of income-maintenance programs, taxes, and regulations on human capital investments. The final section examines entrepreneurship training and the role that it can play in extending opportunity to those with low incomes.

INVESTMENT DECISIONS

In one aspect of our lives—in acquiring education and skills and in marketing ourselves to potential employers—we all act as entrepreneurs. For some this investment activity is concentrated in schooling and job-hunting. For others, the self-employed and those heading their own businesses, the activity is almost continuous. A healthy economy requires a labor force well endowed with basic education and skills, flexibility in the face of change, and the incentives and capacity to pursue entrepreneurial opportunities.

Most individuals make three different types of human capital investment decisions during their working careers. First, they choose what kind of and how much schooling to acquire. (This will depend in large part on their career choice.) Second, individuals must decide how much to invest in job search: should they take the first job offered, should they hold out for a better offer, or should they migrate to an area with better employment opportunities. Finally, they must decide how much on-the-job training to acquire: should they accept a lower paying job that offers training in skills that increase their future earning potential?

These decisions are usually taken with poor information about current labor conditions and even uncertainty about the future and must comply with individuals' resource constraints. Therefore, human capital investments pose some special problems:

1. **Educational investments are relatively costly.** Education is a time-intensive activity, and, despite rising tuition, the opportunity cost of time may easily exceed the out-of-pocket expenses. For example, a two-year associate degree at a community college may cost only $6,000 or $8,000 in fees and expenses but between $15,000 and $20,000 in foregone earnings over two years. Most students work part-time, which lowers foregone earnings. Also the foregone earnings data are a gross measure of the value of sacrificed opportunities because they take no account of the disutility of work.

2. **Educational investments are especially risky because the capital is not liquid.** A skill once acquired may have no "salvage value" should it become obsolete (while most physical capital does have some salvage value). The accumulated knowledge of how to produce steel is of little value when mills are closing. Risk is the absence of information, and many of the critical pieces of data required to predict risks and rewards are unavailable or unreliable.

3. **Educational investments are difficult to finance.** Lending institutions are reluctant to lend to people wishing to finance their education or training because the investments are risky and because skills and education do not offer the lender collateral comparable to that offered in the purchase of physical capital. (If a bank lends for the purchase of a machine, that machine can be resold if the borrower defaults. The future

earnings of a student do not offer comparable security). Therefore, people have to rely on their own assets, those of family and
friends, or government programs. This means that many low-
and middle-income families who lack the savings or income to
pay for education or training will be unable to invest in themselves.

Given the special obstacles to financing investments in human
capital, without government intervention many valuable investments will not be made.

THE GOVERNMENT AS INFORMATION PROVIDER

Acquiring reliable and relevant information about postsecondary
education and training opportunities is difficult. First, the investment decision is not a recurrent one, and so , unlike a firm that is
continually making investment decisions, the individual will invest
correspondingly less in acquiring information. Second, much of the
data that would be of use to the individual—past placement records
of different schools and comparative earnings upon graduation, for
example—is not available to the public. The state collects enormous
files of potentially useful data in the course of administering the
Unemployment Insurance and Social Security programs. Although
the data cannot be released to the public in the form they are collected for reasons of confidentiality, they can be the basis of more
aggregate data that can be released publicly.

If this data is to be collected and distributed, state governments
must do it. In addition to the problem of confidentiality, information
has the characteristic of a collective consumption good—once available to one person, it can be made available at almost no cost to
others. Selling such information may not be profitable, and relying
on market incentives might result in a less than desirable amount of
information being gathered.

Much of the information the government currently provides for
making human capital investment decisions can be misleading. For
example, the employment projections provided by the Bureau of Labor Statistics (BLS) —widely reported in the press and used by high
school and college guidance counselors—are unreliable. In 1970 BLS
predicted that by 1980 there would be 425,000 system analysts. The
actual number was less than half. Again, in 1972, when 3 million

secretaries were employed, BLS projected 4 million by 1980; the actual number was 2.75 million.

Making long-range projections is always risky and, unless the results justify it, is not worthwhile. If proper warnings are not offered and heeded, bad projections can be worse than none at all. While making these long-range projections of variables that cannot be reliably forecast, federal and state governments are failing to collect more current information that would be valuable to decisionmakers and would help people evaluate long-range projections.

Since the past performance of an institution is often a reliable predictor of future performance, the post-graduate employment experience (placement and earnings data) of vocational-technical students would be quite helpful to prospective students in choosing among schools. But not until 1984 did the first state, Florida, mandate the annual reporting of placement rates for all vocational education programs.[4] Arizona is experimenting with a system that will publish, annually, the placement rates and wages for all public and private postsecondary education and training programs.[5] It is vital that both earnings and placement rates are used to measure performance. Reliance on placement rates leads the schools to emphasize short, cheap programs in skills that are easy to place which may not provide participants with the ability to find and keep a good job.[6]

Providing information on labor-market performance of program graduates does not place liberal arts schools at a disadvantage or imply that the sole reason, or even the main reason, for pursuing secondary education is to get a job. There are numerous guides that report on many different characteristics of colleges that help people to make an informed choice. Labor-market data would fill an important gap and the state is in a unique position to fill that gap more effectively and at lower cost than any private organization.

States also administer the Job Service, whose main function is to provide the unemployed with information about employment opportunities. Barely one job out of ten is filled through the service. Most job seekers use newspapers and their own informal channels to find work. The federal funding formula for the Job Service does not encourage the provision of innovative services. However, in 1982 the Wagner-Peyser Act (which established and funds the Job Service) was amended to give states much more discretion over how the funds are used, thus creating opportunities for using the Job Service resources more effectively. For example, in some states the Job Training Partnership program has entered into special contracts with the Job Service to provide placement services for the economically disadvantaged.

GOVERNMENT AS FINANCIER

The importance of government financing of education and training is well established. About half the $250 billion spent each year on education investments comes from public sources—most of it in state and local expenditures.[7] From the full funding of public schools and student loans for graduate students to subsidies for on-the-job training in private firms and the job service, all aspects of the education industry are influenced by a public-sector presence. Most public funds have flowed to institutions, with little attention being given to how well those institutions perform.

There is a strong reason to help those who are poor to finance the acquisition of education and training. Inadequate capital access makes it difficult for many people to borrow to finance education or training. The federal, state, and local response has been to subsidize public educational institutions so that students either pay no admission (kindergarten through twelfth grade) or a greatly subsidized price (vocational education and state universities). Loans, grants, and loan guarantees are also provided to some students, but the level of support to participants is much smaller than the direct support to the colleges and universities they attend.

It will be efficient to subsidize educational institutions rather than individuals only if: 1) institutions have better information concerning employers' needs and individuals' capacities than people themselves; and 2) institutions face greater incentives to meet these demands efficiently. These conditions are rarely met. Schools and universities have no data that they could easily make available to students, and the guarantee of a public subsidy has made many institutions slow to adapt to the changing environment.[8] The benefits of the skills or education acquired accrue to the students, which encourages them to select their program prudently. Students generally have better information on their own talents and aspirations. Overall, the individual has more incentive to invest wisely than does the institution. If the type of information described in the preceding section were available, people would have the data they required to choose among competing educational institutions. If schools and colleges had to compete for students to attract public funds, they might become more responsive in developing new curricula and special programs. Private schools and universities have had to compete and have generally proven more innovative and provided higher quality education.[9]

The current funding system for all levels of education—based primarily on attendance—does not include any incentive for good performance (measured either in terms of increases in student ability or of placement rates and earnings of graduates). A more entrepreneurial environment can be stimulated either by providing public funds to institutions based upon measured performance (as Florida and Arizona are beginning for vocational education) or by providing all funding directly to students and forcing all institutions to compete for this business.[10] The former is a less radical step but lacks the advantage of drawing upon the information possessed by the individual student.

Some observers have recommended that most public support for education should flow to individuals in the form of vouchers—for postsecondary education, training, or for kindergarten to graduate school (with a large part of the aid for higher education being in the form of a guaranteed loan).[11] The vouchers would ensure that everyone could afford an education and could choose where they wished to be educated. The Minnesota legislature, with the governor's support, considered a limited voucher plan for low-income households in 1984.

Proponents believe that competition for students would force institutions to become more innovative and responsive, and that the quality of education would improve. They stress the importance of a comprehensive state program to publish performance data on institutions (such as placement rates and average earnings of graduates, drop-out rates, etc.) so that people could make informed decisions when investing their vouchers.

Opponents believe that there are many issues to be dealt with in designing a voucher system that would determine if it would perform as well as the current system. Would all institutions be privatized? Would the state accredit institutions? Would the state guarantee access of students to institutions? How would learning-disabled people be treated?

The important lessons from this discussion are: 1) although the state must play a role in helping low-income people finance their education and training, government need not own and manage the institutions in which the education is provided; and 2) providing money to institutions without regard for how well they perform creates no incentive for adaptation and improvement. How states deal with their education systems may well be their most important economic development policy.

INCOME MAINTENANCE, TAXATION, AND HUMAN CAPITAL INVESTMENT

Human capital investment decisions are influenced not only by the information and financing available but by many other public policies that indirectly affect the expected risks and returns. These include: income-maintenance programs (which encourage longer job searches leading to better matches between job seeker and job and to reduced labor-force participation); and taxes (which discourage retraining investments).

Income Maintenance

During the past 50 years, Congress and state capitols have enacted a patchwork of programs aimed at guaranteeing food, shelter, and other essential items to everyone regardless of their earned income:[12] These programs exert a powerful influence on the incentives people face to invest in themselves and in their capacity to make those investments. Although federal policies dominate, states administer most programs and have a growing margin of discretion over their implementation. In addition, states must understand how federal policies influence human capital investments in order to design strategies that may mitigate their unintended effects. Workers' compensation "insures" those working against complete loss of income from accident or illness. Unemployment Insurance (UI) and other specialized insurance plans insure against complete loss of income resulting from loss of a job. Welfare insures most citizens against being unable to afford basic necessities. In-kind programs—public housing, Medicaid, food stamps, and social services—supplement basic income-maintenance grants.

These programs reduce the "downside risk" of labor market investments. They cushion individuals from the full consequences of making an unfortunate investment decision or of the sudden devaluation of specific human capital investments. For example, the existence of UI benefits has led to greater investments in job-search activities.[13] The unemployed are able to "hold-out" longer for a more attractive job. This leads to a better match-up between job vacancies and the skills of the employed. However, the increase in time-intensive search investments is at the expense of more "capital intensive" investments in education and training (formal classroom training, for example). UI does not subsidize formal training, and in most states eligibility requirements actively discourage the unemployed from enrolling in full time education and training programs.[14]

The design of welfare programs also discourages human capital investments by participants. Eligibility for welfare, food stamps, and Medicaid declines sharply with income. A welfare recipient who gains a job may face an implicit tax rate of more than 100 percent—

that is, the gain in earned income is more than offset by the loss of transfer payments and in-kind benefits (including eligibility for public housing and Medicaid). Investments in job search and on-the-job training, which would be highly productive from society's viewpoint, are made unattractive to individuals.[15] The fragmented structure of the welfare system means that recertification may take several weeks, which discourages migration of the poor to more promising labor markets. The result is that the poor are trapped in declining areas, while new opportunities are opened to relatively affluent migrants. This reduces wealth production and raises the cost of transfer programs.

A fundamental and irreconcilable dilemma exists in all income-maintenance. We wish to provide "insurance" that is given only to those in need, and income provides the most accessible measure of need. Yet means testing insurance programs discourages investments in human capital. This does not imply that these social programs should be abandoned. It means that the disincentives implicit in them should be recognized, and measures taken to provide stronger incentives for recipients to acquire education, invest in retraining, or expand their job-search.

Tax Disincentives

How taxes affect education and training is unclear. Some education and training investments receive favorable tax treatment: the time-cost of human-capital investments (foregone wages for those enrolled in education and training programs) is automatically expensed; and the capital stock represented by people's skills and education is not subject to state and local property taxes, as is the case with physical capital.[16] On the other hand, the progressive income tax reduces the rewards of investing in further education, tuition costs cannot be depreciated over time (while some physical capital investments actually enjoy a negative tax rate), and those education and training costs that are deductible cannot easily be carried forward to when the investor's higher tax rate increases the value of deductions.

The tax structure discourages workers from investing in new skills. Individuals may only deduct expenses incurred in acquiring skills related to their existing occupations. A steelworker or short-order chef enrolling in technical training for another career cannot deduct tuition fees from current taxable income. This discourages career flexibility and is particularly dysfunctional in view of the growing need for labor retraining. Similarly, job search expenses not related to an individual's current occupation cannot be deducted when computing taxable income.[17]

ENTREPRENEURIAL ASSISTANCE

Human capital includes not only knowledge about academic subjects and about how to use equipment but also knowledge about how to set up and run a business. Most entrepreneurs learn the necessary skills from those already in business or from starting a business and perhaps from failing. Until recently the formal education system has concentrated on teaching business administration. In 1970 only 10 universities offered courses in entrepreneurship. Today 200 do. The growth has been demand driven—of 750 students in a recent class at Harvard Business School, 570 elected to take the school's course on entrepreneurship. State universities have been somewhat slower to adapt than have private universities.[18]

Low-income people have not been offered the same opportunities. For the most part, the poor have been trained for jobs in large, existing corporations. Although not every poor person can escape from dependency by starting a business, the experience of a few programs suggests that there is great potential for entrepreneurship among the poor, and that public programs exist that could harvest this potential.

The Hawaii Entrepreneurship Training and Development Institute (HETADI) has been assisting low-income people start businesses since 1977 and has successfully set up similar programs in Asia and Africa. A not-for-profit corporation funded in part by federal training funds and in part with foundation support, it rigorously screens out about half its applicants by questioning them on their motivation and ideas. It trains only those who have a potentially viable idea and are motivated to pursue it. They are taught by local business people, when possible, and assisted in preparing a plan for the enterprise they wish to start. About half eventually set up a new business, and more than half of those survive—a rate above the average for all new businesses.

In Florida the Broward County CETA program ran a similar program called Be Your Own Boss (BYOB). Again more than half the participants were able to successfully start their own businesses and more than half survived. Women's Economic Development Corporation in Minneapolis—mentioned in Chapter 3—assisted in setting up more than 60 businesses in its first year.

The United Kingdom is conducting a huge public experiment with entrepreneurship. Those unemployed who deposit £1000 in a new business account are provided with a matching grant from the government, £50 per week for a year (slightly less than they would have received had they continued on public assistance), and business advice if they request it. In the last budget year, 50,000 unemployed people took advantage of the scheme (there are more than 3 million unemployed in the United Kingdom), in everything from aerial advertising to horticulture. The results of experiments on a smaller scale had led the British government to believe that there is a large entrepreneurial population among the unemployed that stands an average chance of succeeding. Even with conservative forecasts of success rates, the government estimates that the net cost of the program will be very low.[19]

Many poor people face barriers in setting up their own business because they lack either personal savings or access to people who can finance their project. Many attempts have been made to establish public agencies to make loans to poor or minority businesses at the federal and state level. The problems are great (Chapter 5), and there have been few successes. Even successful programs rarely acquire portfolios of more than 20 or 30 loans—too few to affect the state's entrepreneurial climate significantly.

The examples described above suggest that agencies that provide technical assistance rather than loans or direct investments can encourage entrepreneurship among low-income people effectively and at a fraction of the cost of direct investments. Well-prepared entrepreneurs will have a lower failure rate than those plunging ahead without assistance. However, if the programs are successful in raising the business start-up rate, they will also raise the failure rate. A British official has admitted concern that when the full effects of the massive entrepreneurial experiment are known, the high number of failures will make it difficult to continue the program.

IMPLICATIONS FOR STATE DEVELOPMENT POLICY

What states do about education and training must be a central part of their economic development strategy. How much and how well people invest in education and training will largely determine the rate of economic development. At a time when the importance of human capital is growing, for many, opportunities to acquire it are diminishing. Reductions in federal support for higher education, coupled with the deterioration of programs, demand urgent attention by state policymakers.

The government plays two important roles: information provider and financier. Good information on the performance of institutions is needed to allow people to select what to study and where. But neither federal nor state governments publish this systematically. They have chosen, instead, to concentrate on providing less useful forecasts of occupational demands in the future.

The government must also play a major role in financing education and training investments for low-income households because private lenders cannot. This does not mean, however, that the government must also own and manage the facilities that provide the education. In fact, by financing institutions rather than people, the government has reduced accountability, deterred innovation, and increased overall costs.

States should consider the following initiatives:

- Increased emphasis on funding individuals (through loans and grants) rather than institutions to improve access to education and training programs by those with low-incomes. This could be done by: 1) extending the student loan program to cover additional activities; 2) using Job Training Partnership funds to establish a voucher for remedial education; 3) using WIN money to fund a remedial education voucher program.
- Increased emphasis on measuring the performance of institutions—both placement rates and earnings—and on tying funding to performance.
- Creating a state program to collect, analyze, and distribute performance statistics on all programs in all postsecondary institutions (public and private) to those considering entering a program. This would include the unemployed, employable welfare recipients, and high-school graduates.
- Review education and regulations, especially those that slow the process of curriculum approval and accreditation to encourage greater entrepreneurship among educational institutions; review of labor regulations to identify those that may deter human capital activity (such as the UI restrictions on enrolling in education).
- Identify opportunities to create entrepreneurship programs modeled on those offered by WEDCo or HETADI. These require extensive participation by entrepreneurs and private firms and should not be created as state agencies.

Helping the Displaced

There are two ways of aiding those displaced by the development process: directly compensating those harmed and assisting them to acquire new skills and to find alternative employment.

Compensation. The 3,000 cab medallion owners in New York gain enormously by excluding new entrants (chapter 4). Any expansion of the number of medallions would impose a large capital loss on the value of the medallions they hold. They are prepared to fight tenaciously to protect their monopoly while millions of New Yorkers pay higher cab fares than necessary and cannot get cabs when they need them and those who cannot work as cabdrivers are not as well organized to resist because each of them does not lose as much as a medallion owner gains by perpetuating the monopoly.

To compensate cab companies and drivers for this potential capital loss, Mayor Koch has proposed that additional medallions be issued to existing medallion holders who could sell them if they chose. Even though this offer has thus far been refused by the cab owners, the mayor's offer illustrates that methods can sometimes be devised to reduce the damages experienced by some groups as a result of policy changes.[20]

Compensation is a way of dealing with small and easily identifiable groups of people harmed by development or changing public policy. The gains from plugging special tax loopholes that benefit a few major firms would be greater than the value of those loopholes to the firms, but the change is rarely made. Sometimes the protected benefits are not even financial. Making vocational schools accountable for their performance by making funds contingent on performance measuring has been opposed for many years by school directors, even though most people favor accountability.

Another example of compensation is provided by New York City but is applicable to state policy. In 1981, small manufacturers complained that they were being driven out of their low-cost rental space in Manhattan by landlords anxious to convert the buildings into residential lofts. Pressure mounted to curb conversions that would have slowed development in the city. Instead, the City imposed a small tax on conversions (per square foot of building space) and placed the proceeds in a fund to help defray the cost of relocations for firms, providing they were relocating within New York City. Coal-rich states sometimes use part of the revenues from a state severance tax, for example, to compensate local communities for the fiscal costs of growth.[21]

Redeployment. All economic change causes revaluation of

resources—some increase in value, others decline. For those workers whose skills become redundant or for those entrepreneurs whose firms are overtaken by technological change, the process can be painful—even traumatic. Older workers, those in durable goods manufacturing, and those located in the Northeast experienced the greatest difficulty in finding well-paid jobs during the last decade. In most European countries (and in some American corporations), those laid off permanently are eligible for severance pay that is proportional to seniority. This reflects the special problems that older workers face when they are laid off.

Public officials must be able to respond to the very real problems of those who lose their jobs because of changes in the economy. But federal and state legislation that attempts to delay the change (through import quotas, bailouts, or new regulations, for example) or to provide financial compensation to the losers (increased unemployment benefits, special grants, relocation assistance) can be very expensive.

The programs outlined in the preceding sections would greatly ease the transition problems that confront displaced workers. Improving the entrepreneurial climate will, in the long-run, speed up the process of job generation. Improving the way we finance human capital will make it easier for some of those displaced to acquire the skills demanded in new jobs. But they will not completely eliminate their suffering. Special efforts will be needed to deal with communities hit by a major plant closing in which public service resources may be unable to cope. Several states have programs that detail extra training, education, Unemployment Insurance, job placement, and even mental health staff to a community on a temporary basis.

But nothing the state can do will remove all of the costs. The more the state tries to do, the greater the chance that it may reduce rather than increase economic opportunity.

NOTES

1. Human capital includes not only investments in education and training but also investments that improve health—from jogging to low-cholesterol diets. Only education and training investments are discussed in this chapter. The term was coined by Nobel Laureate economist Theodore Schultz in a seminal book entitled **Investing in Ourselves** published in 1961. He argued that investments in education and skills were as important, if not more important, than investments in physical capital for less-developed countries.

2. Heyne, 1980, p.239. One study of national income between 1975 and 1977 estimated that 85 percent arose from the ownership of human resources (see Heyne, 1980, p.240).

3. Not everyone can acquire the skills needed for a successful entrepreneurial venture for five dollars—which was the cost of learning to make ice-cream for Ben and Jerry (Chapter 2).

   Two hundred years ago, Adam Smith identified the education of those with limited income as an important responsibility of the state (1776, p.736):

   > The education of the common people requires, perhaps, in a civilized and commercial society, the attention of the public more than that of people of some rank and fortune.

4. See Larry Polivka et al., "Performance Based Funding and The Future of Vocational Education", **Entrepreneurial Economy,** March 1985. Florida has since amended the legislation to require the collection of earnings as well as placement rates.

5. See "Training for Tomorrow's Economy: Policies to Improve Skills Training in Arizona," Roger J. Vaughan, governor's Office of Economic Policy and Development, state of Arizona, August 1984. The states control two of the most useful data sources for developing time series data on education and training graduates: the Social Security File and the Unemployment Insurance File. Neither can be released to private firms or people because this would disclose confidential data. But the files can be used to develop time series data on cohorts graduating from education and training programs. These files are the basis of the Arizona and Florida initiatives.

6. The Comprehensive Employment and Training Act encountered problems because it stressed placement rates and did not also analyze the quality of the placements (Taggart, 1981).

7. Accurate figures on expenditures are difficult to compile because there are no reliable data on expenditures by private firms on educating and training their labor force (See the **Digest of Education Statistics: 1983-84,** Washington D.C.: National Center for Education Statistics, 1984.)

8. Vocational education provides a clear example of institutional inertia, caused largely by federal regulations. Between 1920 and 1956, there were virtually no changes in the types of education courses that were eligible for federal funding, despite the transformation of the national economy. Twenty percent of all students were enrolled in agricultural courses (although less than 5 percent of the workforce was in agriculture). Office occupations were not added until 1966. A recent General Accounting Office report documents the widespread abuse of federally funded vocational education programs (U.S. GAO, 1984).

9. See Everhart, 1982.

10. Adam Smith recognized the importance of competition in maintaining the quality of universities and loss of quality that resulted from the provision of state endowments (1776, p.717):

   > The endowments of schools and colleges have necessarily diminished more or less the necessity of application in the teachers. Their subsistence, so far as it arises from their salaries, is evidently derived from a fund altogether independent of their success and reputation in their particular professions...

   > The charitable foundations of scholarships, exhibitions, bursarships etc., necessarily attach a certain number of students to certain colleges, independent altogether of the merit of these particular colleges.

> Were the students upon such charitable foundations left free to chuse [sic] what college they liked best, such liberty might perhaps contribute to excite some emulation among different colleges.

11. See the work of Doyle and Finn (1984) and, for a discussion of the many issues in this important policy debate, Everhart, 1982. Some people approve of vouchers for post-secondary education because individuals are able to choose where to pursue their education, while children attending kindergarten through twelfth grade must go where their parents select.

12. By far the largest of these—the complex of programs collectively referred to as Social Security—is not intended to help those experiencing difficulties in the labor market, although the availability of benefits has undoubtedly encouraged early retirement (particularly among those in low-wage jobs).

13. Ehrenberg and Oaxaca, 1976.

14. Federal regulations give state administrators some flexibility such as allowing enrollment upon approval by the state head of the department of labor (or whichever agency administers the UI system). Few states have chosen to market this option to beneficiaries aggressively.

15. Some states have tried to lower the implicit tax rate. For example, in its Temporary Employment Assistance Program New York State ensures that those welfare recipients who are hired by a private employer as part of the program retain Medicaid eligibility (O'Neill, 1985).

16. Most investments in long-lived assets are deducted not when the asset is purchased but as it is used up over time. For example, investments in business capital can be written off over 15, 5, or 3 years. Expensing allows the full cost to be written off immediately.

17. There is some logic to these rules. The IRS does not wish to subsidize perpetual students or vacations masquerading as job searches. But in the process of preventing abuse, the tax code also excludes genuine investment expenses.

18. See Gumpert and Timmons, 1982.

19. The government believes that taxes paid by successful entrepreneurs and reduction in public assistance payments will be more than the government's investments in the new business accounts. This is, of course, not an estimate of the net social value of the program.

20. So far the cab medallion owners have not accepted the Mayor's offer.

21. These programs are discussed in greater detail in Vaughan, 1983, Chapter 5.

CHAPTER 7

INVESTING IN PUBLIC CAPITAL

> [To government belongs] the duty of erecting and maintain-
> ing certain public works and certain public institutions,
> which it can never be for the interest of any individual or
> small number of individuals, to erect and maintain; because
> the profit could never repay the expense to any individual or
> small number of individuals, though it may frequently do
> much more than repay it to a society.
>
> Adam Smith (1776, Vol.II, p. 185)

Infrastructure—transportation networks, water supply and treatment systems, and other public facilities—is necessary for economic
development. The level and quality of infrastructure investments and
the effectiveness of maintenance programs influence the growth potential of a state's economy and its ability to respond to a changing
environment.

The state's involvement in the investment process is greater for
public works investments than for business and human capital. It
not only finances the investments, it also selects the projects, often
retains ownership of the facility, and is responsible for operating and
maintaining it.

Yet public works investments have been neglected by many
states that are constrained by tight budgets. The share of GNP invested in public works declined from 5 percent in 1965 to only 2
percent in 1985.[1] Seventeen percent of the nation's bridges are in
"critical or basically intolerable condition." Some major cities lose
nearly half of their water through water-main leaks. Not only have
states cut spending, but they have not developed planning and budgeting procedures to ensure that public investments are made wisely.

The first section of this chapter discusses the nature of public
works investments and why they are publicly undertaken. The section describes the problems of acquiring the information needed for
selecting projects when the services they provide are not explicitly
priced to users. The second section discusses the principles to apply
in assigning responsibility for public works projects between public
and private sectors. The third section discusses how public works
can be more effectively planned and budgeted, even in the absence of
the types of direct data that guide private investment. The fourth
section examines financing issues, arguing that increased reliance
on user fees provides a stronger basis for financing than general tax

revenues and also provides decisionmakers with better data on needed investments.

WHY ARE PUBLIC WORKS PUBLIC

In theory, infrastructure investments have become a public responsibility because there are no ways of collecting revenues from beneficiaries that would cover the costs of the investments, even though their actual value exceeds those costs. For example, it would be so cumbersome to charge each user of a street that it is easier to finance roads and sidewalks through a general property tax. In reality, political considerations also have encouraged the public funding of major construction projects. Because politicians represent specific locales, public subsidies for projects with very specific impacts are attractive. From Boss Tweed's courthouse to today's domed stadium, political tests have become as important as the market test of willingness to pay in judging public works projects. In the eighteenth century, Adam Smith noted the susceptibility of public works to political manipulation. He correctly identified the root of the problem as the ability to use general tax revenues rather than require the project be financed out of user fees (1776, p.683):

> A great bridge cannot be thrown across the river at a place where nobody passes, or merely to embellish the view from the windows of a neighboring palace: things which sometimes happen, in countries where works of this kind are carried on by any other revenue than that which they themselves are capable of affording.

Even without political pressure, evaluating public projects is difficult. The decisionmaker does not have accurate information from which to estimate the benefits of a proposed investment. A private enterprise can use sales, costs, and profit data to predict the value of a proposed investment—subject, of course, to uncertainty over future market conditions. The public investor has no such data.

The most important decision a state must make is how to allocate responsibilities between the public and private sectors. This is discussed in the following section. Savings made from turning over responsibility for water supply or waste-water treatment projects to private companies are large. Savings made from better planning, budgeting, and financing procedures are even larger.

Rigorous capital budgeting is the only way that the "market" test for public works can be strengthened relative to the political test. This makes capital budgeting difficult to introduce in a state that has a strong tradition of public pork-barrelling. Preparing a capital budget does not mean that all public works decisions should be made through rigorous cost-benefit analysis. If the value of the project can be easily computed, it may be appropriate to turn it over to private enterprise. In most cases, cost-benefit analysis will not yield an unambiguous conclusion because many aspects of large-scale construction projects, such as environmental impacts and income distribution consequences, do not lend themselves to quantification. These aspects are sometimes better dealt with through the political process, which allows for a broader array of factors to be considered.

Private market decisions are made on the basis of one dollar one vote. The intensity of feeling as well as the wealth of individuals' preferences are reflected in how much they are prepared to pay. Both parties have to agree to a transaction before a deal can be struck. In governmental decisionmaking, each person is accorded a vote, regardless of wealth, and can express the intensity of his or her feelings on issues by contributing to and participating in special interest groups. This makes the political process particularly suitable for decisions that involve strong nonmarket elements such as redistribution and environmental quality. A deal can be struck with a bare majority agreeing, which makes it easier to reach agreement on complex issues.[2]

ASSIGNING RESPONSIBILITY

The legitimate object of government is to do for people what needs to be done, but which they cannot by individual effort do at all, or do so well for themselves.

Abraham Lincoln (1858)

There is no simple rule to determine who should do what in our economy. Private entrepreneurs tend to be the most effective decisionmakers in those parts of the economy characterized by uncertainty, rapid change, and wide variation in consumer tastes. The public sector tends to be better at decisionmaking in those areas characterized by external effects, strong distributional impacts, and conflicting values.

As a basic principle, the public sector should perform only those tasks that the private sector cannot perform at all or as well or where competition from the public sector can contribute to innovative behavior. Adhering to this principle provides economic opportunities for private enterprise and forces states to concentrate their fiscal and administrative resources on those activities in which they have a comparative advantage. They have not always done so.

For nearly two decades, as state budgets were expanding and economic development programs were multiplying, states under-invested in public works and allowed their education systems to deteriorate. An increase in public responsibilities was not the only nor even the main cause of either of these problems. But had more fiscal resources and administrative attention been available, public works would have been better maintained, and education would have been less neglected.

The selection of those activities in which states have an advantage must be based on judgment and experience. They must also be made with reference to the legal and institutional traditions and the public's tastes for collective goods. In the past, states have gradually taken over activities such as mass transportation, health care, education, and low income housing (mostly with the legal and fiscal encouragement of the federal government). In some places, it has taken over the financing of dry-docks, hotels, and even sports stadia. But in recent years the trend has reversed and privatization has become popular, particularly as federal programs have been cut and as evidence mounts that private firms are, in many instances, able to provide services at lower cost than public agencies.[3]

The criteria for deciding whether a good or service would be more effectively supplied by the private sector are:

- Do private incentives reflect social benefits and costs? Are there externalities that businesses will not take into account? Is it reasonable to exclude nonpayers from using a good or service?
- Do entrepreneurs have better information for finding and evaluating opportunities than the government?

In many instances, such as education, housing, mass transit, and health care, government has assumed responsibility on the grounds that some consumers could not afford adequate service. Thus bus fares are subsidized to allow those with low incomes to ride, free admission to parks is allowed, and free primary education is provided through local school boards.

There are alternative ways of assisting the poor without resorting to complete public ownership and operation. The desire to provide facilities and services to those with low incomes requires public financing but not public production. As the gas lines in 1979 showed, subsidizing people through the price system is very costly. Instead of producing services, the state could provide low-income households, or even all households, with vouchers that encourage the competitive provision of services by private firms. Vouchers are used to encourage adequate dietary habits by those with low incomes; a large-scale housing voucher experiment showed that the quality of shelter of those with low incomes can be improved by providing vouchers instead of building public housing (see reports by the Rand Corporation). Several state legislatures are considering the use of tuition vouchers as a way of encouraging the more efficient provision of education (Chapter 6).[4]

CAPITAL PLANNING AND BUDGETING

Cuts in state spending on public works are only partly responsible for the deteriorated state of much of the nation's infrastructure. Inadequate or misconceived capital planning and budgeting practices, shortsighted management policies, and inappropriate project evaluation procedures must bear a large part of the blame. For example, it has proven politically expedient, whenever state revenues fall, to defer maintenance of infrastructure rather than lay off teachers or policemen, even though this may be economically unwise. State budgets do not show the costs of deferring maintenance, and attention has not been focused on the issue until a series of well-publicized and tragic accidents.

Effective planning and budgeting requires, first, a mechanism for assessing public works needs; and second, a logical way for evaluating alternative projects.

Needs Assessment

A major obstacle to identifying the most productive infrastructure projects is a lack of information on: 1) the current condition of existing facilities, and 2) the demands that are likely to be made on them in the future.

Condition Assessment. Recent investigations have shown how little information states have concerning the condition of the public works for which they are responsible. To remedy this, several states have conducted systematic assessments or inventories of their public facilities. For example, Washington State's Planning and Community Affairs Agency conducted a comprehensive survey in 1982. They distributed 700 surveys to the state's cities, counties, and special purpose districts. The responses, which covered 98 percent of the population, provided planners with 800,000 pieces of information on the conditions of the state's public works. These will be used to identify the highest priority projects in the future.

Condition assessment must rely heavily on the personal judgment of the survey respondents. For facilities such as roads and bridges, more objective guidelines have been developed. Over time, experience with this procedure should lead to the development of more objective standards for other types of public works.

Relying on personal judgment can distort results. Local jurisdictions will report a bleaker picture than actually prevails if they believe that this will lead to greater state assistance. To discourage misrepresentation, survey respondents in Washington State were informed that their responses would be published and open to public scrutiny.

States need not perform a comprehensive assessment every year. Once a data base is established, assessments need be performed every few years, or only a sample of jurisdictions need be surveyed annually.

Demand Assessment.   When the State of California performed a needs assessment, the City of Irvine reported that it needed another library and a civic center. Yet if these facilities were really needed, why had the city not built them itself? Obviously the needs were not sufficiently urgent to merit spending local money. If its money is involved in financing priority investments, the state must find a way of measuring the urgency of needs. Urgency is captured in the economic notion of "demand," which relates items that are desired to the sacrifices people are willing to make to acquire them.

Predicting future infrastructure demands requires long-range forecasts of population and economic activity—magnitudes that cannot be reliably forecast very far into the future. Expensive models do not necessarily add greater precision. A consensus forecasting approach such as that used by Florida may be a useful and low-cost appproach. It uses judgmental forecasts by thoughtful and knowledgeable people who meet regularly and ensure that all agencies use the same forecast.

States can accommodate some uncertainty in their pubic works planning. Temporary facilities may be erected when doubt exists about the future demand for a facility, or a project's timing can be conditioned upon crossing threshold levels of demographic and economic indicators.

There is no right way to predict demand. What is important is to establish a formal process that blends whatever data can be generated with the judgment of experienced people meeting together.

Project Evaluation[5]

The object of project evaluation is to provide a framework within which to organize information about the pros and cons of a project. Ideally projects would be compared according to their **net benefits** (or net present value)—the excess of project benefits over costs. This is the single indicator that measures the addition to community wealth that can be expected if the project is undertaken. However, it is rarely possible to predict or measure all the pros and cons, and therefore project evaluation becomes a process of assigning those impacts that can be measured as either a benefit or a cost, and determining ways of approximating missing data.

Applying the principles of project evaluation to actual investments can be a formidable task because:

- There are countless investment alternatives from which to choose. Any cracked road or leaking pipe is a candidate for replacement investment, not to mention the multitude of new projects that different constituencies would like to see undertaken.
- Public-works projects may take several years to complete and provide benefits far into the future. Predicting the benefits and costs of a specific project can prove difficult. They may depend on climatological patterns, demographic factors, or on regional economic growth—elements difficult to forecast far into the future.
- Critical information may be unavailable. Because many public facilities are provided free of charge or at subsidized prices, the information about values that private firms gain from market prices is not available for most public projects.

Project-evaluation techniques cannot eliminate uncertainty, but properly applied the principles of project evaluation should produce the best-educated guesses. Three basic principles should not be ignored:

1. **The true cost of resources used in a project is their opportunity cost or their value in their best alternative use.** The cost of a water treatment plant, for example, includes the value of what that labor, concrete, steel and land could have produced as roads, buildings, or whatever is their best alternative use. The opportunity cost of a resource is not necessarily what was paid for it so budgetary costs may differ from opportunity costs.[6]

2. **Future benefits should be discounted.** The fact that interest must be paid to borrow money indicates that people prefer goods today to the same amount of goods available sometime in the future. A highway completed this year is obviously more valuable than one completed several years from now. Even without inflation, a dollar's worth of project benefits available one year from now is worth less than that dollar of benefits today.[7] A serious limitation of capital budgeting is that there is no simple rule prescribing what interest rate should be used to discount future benefits. There are, however, some rules-of-thumb that can be used.[8] Nevertheless, undiscounted estimates will generally be less useful than discounted ones.

3. **Risky benefits should be discounted.** The predicted benefits of resurfacing a heavily used highway are almost certain to materialize, but the benefits of building a new light-rail system, a new convention center, or an industrial park may not. Some public works are risky in that there is a high possibility that their benefits will fall short of their expected level. On the whole people are averse to risk; larger rewards must be offered to attract investors to risky projects. Therefore, the expected net benefits of public works projects should be discounted to reflect the degree of risk—the riskier the project, the higher the discount rate.[9]

Rules-of-Thumb for Making Public Investment Decisions.

It is impractical to perform project evaluations for every proposed capital expenditure; many are too small to warrant such an investment and others are too similar to projects already executed to merit repeating a time-consuming procedure. Other methods may be more appropriate. For recurring investments, such as resurfacing of roads or replacing water mains, rules-of-thumb or **decisionmaking algorithms** are usually more suitable.

In the past state and local governments have relied upon engineering algorithms that take no account of whether a procedure is economically sound. Establishing conditions that determine when certain classes of assets must be repaired or replaced eliminates the need to analyze each case. Decision-making algorithms conserve scarce budget and planning staff resources. The algorithms are based on the principles of project evaluation and can only be used when records of past performance are available (and when past performance is a dependable predictor of future performance). For example, by analyzing previous water-main breaks, the City of New

York was able to develop a replacement strategy that accomplished the same reduction in breaks at a third of the cost of the previous procedure.

Capital Budgeting

The capital budget translates the capital plan into action. The budget records where the state has spent and plans to spend large sums of money, shows how the state's fixed assets are depreciating, and projects where the state intends to get the money. For many activities, a comparison of actual expenditures with budget targets measures the performance of capital construction and maintenance programs. The budget is a vital planning tool because it contains, in condensed form, a great deal of information on investments. A capital budget is also a constant reminder of the magnitude and importance of infrastructure investments.

To provide the greatest possible benefits, states should consider developing a comprehensive capital budget document that would include the following information for every major project:

- A project description, reference, and classification.
- Expenditure information.
- Project-evaluation information.
- Projected impact of future operating and maintenance expenditures on operating budgets.
- Financing options.
- Net cost of deferral for one year.

Capital budgeting has the potential to improve the effectiveness of public works investments and stretch infrastructure dollars. Whether these benefits will be realized depends ultimately on the commitment by the governor, planners, and the general public.

FINANCING PUBLIC WORKS

State and local governments draw upon four sources of finance for public works: they borrow against general revenues or against specific revenue sources (user fees or charges); they receive grants from higher levels of government; and they encourage private-sector participation for all or part of the project.

There is no correct formula for financing infrastructure. Federal or state grants can ease the burden on local governments that will have to do most of the planning, but they can also distort priorities, causing jurisdictions to invest in those projects for which grant funds are available at the expense of other more worthy projects. Debt financing may be suitable for one jurisdiction while constitutionally prohibited in another. Like capital planning and budgeting, every state and local government must tailor its financing strategy according to its needs and within its unique legal and institutional environment. The following principles, however, can serve as a general guide for financing decisions:[10]

- Whenever possible the beneficiaries of a public facility should pay for its development and operation. Payments should be related to the level of use.
- The cost of a public capital project should be amortized over the life of the project, and maintenance and operating costs should not be deferred.
- The operating and maintenance expenses associated with a project—operating a convention center, maintaining a bridge, or repairing and upgrading a resource recovery center—should be explicitly considered when designing the financing package.
- Fiscal and administrative responsibility for a public investment project should fall to those jurisdictions most affected by the project.

With these principles in mind, some specific ways that states can reduce the overall cost of financing public works are examined.

Reducing the Cost of Borrowing

State and local governments rely heavily on tax-exempt debt to support their capital investments. The amount of money raised through the municipal bond market usually accounts for 20 to 25 percent of state and local capital spending. Outstanding debt of state and local governments increased by 158 percent between 1970 and 1981. But rising interest rates have driven up the cost of borrowing. Interest costs on debt represented 4 percent of total state spending in 1981, compared with about 1 percent in 1964. There are a number of measures states can take to minimize their borrowing costs.

First, states can strengthen their collateral. The soundness or quality of a bond is determined by a number of objective factors—its maturity, its repayment provisions, and the repayment capacity generated by the project—over which the state exercises some control. The project's or jurisdiction's overall revenue base, its legal and institutional environment, and its ability to plan and manage all enter

into investors' evaluations and can be viewed as the borrowing entity's collateral. Strengthening these enhances the debt's market-
ability.

Second, states can carefully choose the type of debt used to
finance a project. For projects generating revenue streams, they can
rely on revenue bond financing, thus reserving their general obli-
gation financing for those projects for which no alternative source of
financing is possible.

Third, states can use more efficient revenue sources to back
debt. Debt can be serviced by general taxes (income, sales, and property taxes); dedicated revenues (gasoline taxes, earmarked lottery
revenues, and severance taxes); user fees (metered water charges,
road tolls, park entrance fees, and tuition fees); and intergovernmental transfers (grants and loans from one level of government to another). Structuring the most efficient revenue stream to
back debt is part of building collateral. The advantages and disad-
vantages of each form of revenue are discussed below.

General Taxation.   At first glance, general tax support looks like a
good idea. By relying on a wider range of taxes rather than on one or
two dedicated sources and by spreading the tax burden across the
entire population rather than imposing it on a narrow group of
users, a jurisdiction can cushion the risk. But this masks a number
of problems. First, income and sales taxes are vulnerable during
economic downturns, which threatens the security of the repayment
promise. Second, general tax appropriations are subject to political
pressures. While the legislature might channel a certain portion of
overall tax revenues to service this year's debt, there is no guarantee
that future legislatures will make the same decision. Third, by disas-
sociating the payment for the service from its use, taxpayers are
more inclined to be wasteful consumers. Finally, it is difficult to raise
general taxes.

Dedicated Revenues.   Revenues earmarked to service long-term
debt are less vulnerable to political pressures. They can guarantee
that funds will be set aside to service the debt and pay for needed
maintenance and repair for a specified period of time. Dedicated
revenues do not necessarily encourage more efficient use of public
services, however. Colorado, for example, dedicates 50 percent of the
net revenues from its state lottery for capital projects. This guarantees a stream of funds for public works but does not influence how
these facilities and services are used.

User Fees:[11]   User fees are essentially dedicated revenues in that
they are earmarked for specific capital investments. User fees can
have the added advantage of encouraging more efficient use of facil-

111

ities because the revenues paid are linked to the level of use. Prices that are set at the opportunity cost of providing the service or maintaining the facility serve two purposes. They encourage consumers to carefully weigh the value of every increment of use against the use of alternative goods and services. Second, suppliers of the service have the benefit of more accurate information as to whether to expand, reduce, or maintain existing levels of service. Not all user fees, however, are structured efficiently. Declining block rates provide incentives for inefficient use of services in that they price each increment of service at a lower rate as more are used. User fees are viewed with some reluctance because they are thought to be inequitable. However, a properly structured fee system can be both equitable and efficient.[12]

Intergovernmental Transfers. Grants are simply a redistribution of general tax revenues collected by one level of government and awarded to another. Because they are supported by general revenues, they are vulnerable to all the problems mentioned earlier: they are cut when the economy turns down; grants frequently cause a community to defer its own spending for needed projects; and they often require local matching funds, which channels revenues away from higher priority projects. Finally, grants tend to pay only for new construction—maintenance and repairs are not covered and are often not done, which results in waste.

IMPLICATIONS FOR STATE DEVELOPMENT POLICY

The political process provides a way of making decisions on large scale and complex projects that are characterized by large distributional effects and significant unpriceable impacts. However, governmental decisions are often made with too little regard for the long-term economic consequences. The infrastructure part of a state development strategy should have three components: 1) a process for identifying services and facilities that could be built and operated more cheaply by private enterprise; 2) a more rigorous capital planning and budgeting process that would help restore some market considerations into infrastructure decisions; and 3) changes in financing methods that would include a greater reliance on dedicated revenues and user fees to provide more predictable funding and better information for planning.

Policies for Assigning Responsibilities[13]

These include:

1. Establish a small division in either the Budget Office or the Department of Administration to evaluate opportunities for using private enterprises to provide goods and services currently provided by the state or by local governments.
2. Review state legislation that may limit the powers of local authorities to use private enterprise.
3. Provide state technical assistance to localities in developing contracts and monitoring performance of private vendors.

Policies to Improve Planning, Budgeting, and Financing Public Works

Infrastructure and education are two of the largest components of state spending. They offer the potential for large budget savings in return for the adoption of measures that would improve the way in which investments are selected, financed, and managed. Nothing may be more important for state development policy than the way it conducts the activities for which it has assumed responsibility. Measures that could improve public infrastructure investments include:

1. Long-term planning and the preparation of an annual capital budget;
2. Improved maintenance and management procedures;
3. Increased reliance on user charges, earmarked revenues, and other financing methods that would ensure the long-term commitment of funds and produce useful information for planners and managers. The powers of local governments to employ these types of financing methods should be broadened.
4. Reduction and ultimate elimination of programs providing local governments with grants to pay for public works—grants encourage the construction of facilities that the local government is not prepared to pay for.
5. Ensuring that private developers pay the full cost of utility hookups and additional public facilities needed in a new development.

NOTES

1. For a description of the symptoms of the infrastructure problem, as well as its causes, see Vaughan, 1983 and Vaughan and Pollard, 1984.

2. Some decisions require approval of two thirds or three quarters of those voting. Usually these are decisions involving fundamental changes in constitutional matters.

3. When public and private sectors compete in the delivery of services such as solid-waste collection, health care, public transportation, and fire protection, empirical evidence indicates that private vendors are consistently cheaper (Savas, 1983, Smith, 1985, De Alessi, 1975, and Zimmerman, 1977). Bennett and Johnson (1980) reviewed many studies and concluded:

   > Without exception, the empirical findings indicate that the same level of output could be produced at substantially lower costs if output were produced by the private rather than the public sector.

4. Adam Smith offered a simple solution to those that claimed the poor could not afford the user fees of properly priced public services (1776, p.683):

   > When the toll upon the carriages of luxury, upon coaches, post-chaises, and so on, is made somewhat higher in proportion to their weight, than upon carriages of necessary use, such as carts, waggons, and so on, the indolence and vanity of the rich is made to contribute in a very easy manner to the relief of the poor, by rendering cheaper the transportation of heavy goods to all the different parts of the country.

5. An excellent and practical discussion is provided in Gramlich, 1981.

6. For example, a proposed park may be sited on land already owned by the state. But that does not mean the cost of using it as a park is nothing. At the very least, the state could have sold the land or perhaps used it as a wilderness area, a resource-recovery site, or a state health care facility. The value of the land in the most valuable of these alternatives determines its opportunity cost.

7. Public works investments vary widely in their construction periods and useful lives. To compare the net benefits of these projects effectively, all dollars must be measured at the same time. The simplest way to accomplish this is to discount all dollars of benefits and costs to the present to get the **present value** of the project's net benefits.

8. See Vaughan and Pollard, 1984, p.47ff.

9. Because risk is difficult to measure and forecast, only crude and somewhat arbitrary adjustments can be made. Nevertheless, an imperfect adjustment for risk is usually superior to none at all. In general, the benefits from building a new facility whose demand is very difficult to estimate should be discounted more heavily than those from repairing or replacing an existing facility whose past history makes demand easier to forecast.

10. See Vaughan, 1983, Chapter 4.

11. Adam Smith was a powerful advocate of user fees and believed that they need not impose an unnecessary burden on the poor (1776, p.682):

    > It does not seem necessary that the expence of those public works should be defrayed from public revenue, as it is commonly called, of which the collection and application are in most countries assigned to the executive power. The greater part of such public works may easily be so managed, as to afford a particular revenue sufficient for defraying their own expence, without bringing any burden upon the general revenue of society.

A highway, a bridge, a navigable canal, for example may in most cases be both made and maintained by a small toll upon the carriages that use them: a harbour, by a moderate port-duty upon the tonnage of shipping which load or unload in it.

12. A detailed analysis of the advantages of user fees in financing water projects is contained in Smith, 1985.

13. Some of the policy issues are discussed in greater detail in Vaughan and Pollard, 1984, and Smith, 1985.

PART 3: THE POLITICAL ECONOMY

CHAPTER 8

THE POLITICAL ECONOMY OF STATE DEVELOPMENT POLICY

> Ninety percent of the political art lies in ostentatious giving and surreptitious taking.
>
> Thomas Sowell (1981, p.26)

Carrying out the type of entrepreneurial strategy outlined in the previous chapters is not easy. There is no organized constituency for entrepreneurship. Entrepreneurs are dispersed throughout the state in all communities and in all industries and are usually found outside traditional organizations. The term "entrepreneur" is poorly understood. It carries many different political connotations—Republicans use it as an answer to the New Deal, and Democrats use it to describe the "neo-liberal" agenda. Finally, entrepreneurship is a long term strategy that does not conform to the political imperative of providing visible evidence of success within an election timetable.

Yet the pressure to do something about the economy remains, even though no consensus exists over what that something should be. The constituency for state development policy continues to grow. It includes factory workers about to lose their jobs as imports grow; businesses that lobby to retain special privileges; businesses that threaten to leave the state unless the same privileges are afforded them; owners of small and minority businesses who demand sheltered contracts from the state; declining businesses that expect special loans; and construction workers who ask for extra public works jobs programs.

Yet this type of strategy is not impossible. It does not require abandoning existing programs and their constituents. It does require broadening development policy to encompass activities that in the past may not have been viewed as development policy, including public works, education, and many branches of regulatory policy. Some traditional development policies may have to be reformed—the state may not have sufficient resources to continue large tax abatement programs, for example. But the new strategy should build upon the strengths of current efforts.

The strategy need not conflict with social goals such as the alleviation of poverty, the expansion of opportunities for minorities, or environmental protection. Indeed, many of the policies that would be included in an entrepreneurial strategy both encourage development and assist the economically disadvantaged. For example, state actions that encourage banks to make slightly riskier loans would benefit those who have not been able to borrow in the past because they had insufficient personal resources or lived in a risky neighborhood. Because the economically disadvantaged are frequently the victims of unnecessary restrictions on economic activity, they would constitute a disproportionate percentage of those benefiting from the types of initiatives described in the preceding chapters.[1]

But if development policy is to be successfully expanded, the state's strategy must be pragmatic and coupled with a vigorous public communication program. This can be done in three steps: first, clearly identify and publicize the economic problems confronted; second, put together the legislative and executive initiatives that comprise the strategy; and third, educate the public about the merits of the proposed actions, building support for coalitions and retaining the support of established constituents. This chapter discusses these steps in turn.

STEP 1: DEFINE THE PROBLEM

At any given time, a state confronts many problems. Highways deteriorate, school achievement scores fall, plants close, and people are unemployed. Moreover, the state economy will be buffeted by forces over which it exercises no control—federal policy changes, technological progress, and shifting patterns of world trade. Development will continue to create dislocations as well as opportunities. No strategy can hope to cure all problems, however carefully designed or fervently supported.

Therefore, it is essential that the problem be properly identified and clearly communicated, that the strategy be focused on that aspect of the problem that is "manageable," that the solution be comprehensible, and that successes be measured and clearly and frequently communicated to the public. It is also important to establish what issues the state will not address.

Select the Right Problems

A state's development strategy should target a problem with well-defined characteristics. First, it must be important and comprehensible enough to command public attention. It is difficult to stimulate a busy legislature into action on an issue that affects only a tiny fraction of the state's workforce or that cannot be summarized to the public in a few sentences.

Second, it should not disappear of its own accord. Cyclical problems and self-correcting problems (such as fiscal surpluses or shortages of engineers) should not be the focus of long-run development programs.

Finally, the issue should not have been the focus of recent initiatives that were poorly received. If a past program aimed at "putting the poor in jobs" or "rebuilding the state infrastructure" were poorly received because they were overpromised, badly designed, or ineptly managed, a new program that attempts to cover the same ground will not be well received politically and will fall into the same trap as its predecessor.

Publicize the Problem

Helping to shape the public's perception of economic problems and to clarify the state role in addressing them is difficult but essential. An entrepreneurial strategy will require much more communication than a traditional development strategy because the necessary avenues of communication have not been opened up.

A first step is to involve the governor's communications director/press secretary from the start. Often the communications director is not brought in until the last moment to write the appropriate material for the press announcing the governor's new initiative. Being involved early, the communications director can help design the strategy in a way that makes it easier to explain to the public. A good communications director has regular contact with the media and knows how the public will react to issues.

The second step is to develop a crisp graphic presentation of the issue to provide to the media. Often reporters will use this material directly. Florida's communications director, for example, provides the press with charts and graphic presentations on key state issues. For the last several years, the papers in the state have used the graphics supplied to explain the state's budget.

Third, establish gubernatorial commissions, special task forces, or legislative hearings to examine the problem. Several states used this approach to convey the importance of the infrastructure crisis. They were able to convert the public concern that they aroused into successful passage of bond referenda, increases in dedicated tax revenues, and greater state spending. Michigan appointed a special "blue ribbon" commission in 1976 to investigate its chronic fiscal crises and was able to enact a comprehensive stabilization fund and tax restructuring in spite of opposition from the largest established industries. Colorado appointed a prestigious panel to examine what the state needed to do to confront the problems caused by its rapid growth and therefore established widespread support for long term capital planning.

Problems should not, however, be discovered too frequently. Marketing an education crisis in the spring, an economic crisis in the summer, and an infrastructure crisis in the fall will tire the legislature and the public and confuse agencies about the chief executive's priorities and their own responsibilities.

STEP 2: BUILD THE STRATEGY

> Government produces the infrastructure of society—legal, physical, educational, from highways through skills—that is the precondition of wealth . . . Investment must be made in people before they can be socially competent. And it is obvious, once you think about it, that government is, and must be, a major investor.
>
> George Will (1983, p.125)

Without a clear set of principles to determine what the state should and should not do, the chief executive has no way of rejecting the pleas of some and accepting those of others without appearing unfair. Also, without such principles there is the danger of being drawn into a "sure loser" issue over which the state exerts little or no control. Many severe economic problems, such as the decline of employment in basic industries, would require massive federal action to arrest. Any state strategy that promised to solve such problems is likely to fail.

The state's strategy must, therefore, be based on identifying not only the problems confronting the state economy but the extent of the state government's responsibilities in addressing those problems.

States must assemble their development strategies by selecting from many potential initiatives. Some programs will be included because they provide a visible indicator of the state's commitment to economic development such as state promotional efforts, recruitment programs, and, perhaps, some mild tax abatement programs. But the ultimate success of the strategy will depend upon selecting policies that stimulate development.

The preceding chapters have described the reasons for pursuing certain initiatives to encourage economic development. The initiatives fall into four areas: 1) improving the environment to entrepreneurship, in which the emphasis is upon reducing the barriers to entry to industries and occupations and streamlining regulations; 2) improving the availability of capital for business investment by regulatory and tax measures that encourage competition in the financial sector and risk investments; 3) more effective financing of education and training based on a stronger emphasis on funding people rather than institutions and on providing better information on labor-market and training opportunities; and 4) better planning, budgeting, and financing of public works.

However, there are limits to how many legislative initiatives a package can contain without creating confusion and weakening its chances of success. There are also limits to how many administrative initiatives can be successfully carried out by a bureaucracy. Attractive and politically viable initiatives must often be foregone because administering agencies will lack the staff to carry out the program. It is usually easier to enact legislation that increases the powers and responsibilities of agencies than to pass a budget appropriation to pay for additional staff.

Finally, it is vital that the public and the legislature view the strategy as a package. Each part must be seen as necessary to the success of the whole. If parts can be attacked individually, then the whole strategy may be picked apart by a hostile legislature. Balancing policies to assist the displaced can temper opposition to measures that may accelerate the pace of development. Sometimes goring all oxen gives an appearance of impartiality that weakens opposition.

STEP 3: BUILD SUPPORT

The economist in government must recognize that in formulating any public policy there are political opportunity costs to be considered equally as real and as important as economic opportunity costs.

Charles Schultze (1982)

There are four elements to building support: 1) provide visible evidence of success; 2) educate the public about the importance of entrepreneurship to the state's economy; 3) retain the support of existing groups, many of whom may feel threatened by the prospect of greater competition and new business development; 4) build new coalitions of those who would benefit from the new strategy.

Evidence of Success

The public is easily persuaded that state government does little to help matters. Therefore, it is imperative to identify measures of the success of the program and announce these goals in advance. For some policies, these measures are fairly straightforward. Repairing the state's infrastructure can be defined in terms of bridges repaired and miles of road resurfaced, for example. For other programs, measures are more elusive. A program to reduce dependence by increasing the self-sufficiency of women or older workers is less easy to evaluate.

Many of the policies suggested in the preceding chapters are important but influence the economy indirectly. If banks are successfully encouraged to make slightly riskier loans, it will not be possible to identify which businesses are the beneficiaries.[2] In these cases, less direct measures have to be employed. The list below suggests some measures, direct and indirect, for development strategies:

Measures for a strategy to promote new business might include:

- An increase in the rate of new business formation;
- The number of firms in the state making **Inc**'s 500;
- Publicizing local inventions or innovations (a "Governor's Entrepreneurial Awards" program);

Measures for a strategy to repair the state's infrastructure might include:

- Percent increase in roads resurfaced annually;
- Percent reduction in the cost per mile of resurfacing;
- Number of fewer vehicle accidents attributable to roadway conditions;
- Percent increase in life expectancy of state office buildings due to improved maintenance;

Measures for an education strategy might include:

- Increase in average teacher qualifications;
- Increase in achievement scores;
- Reductions in drop-out rates;
- Numbers of merit scholars;

Measures of a strategy to reduce dependency might include:

- Numbers employed through the program (together with estimates of the fiscal savings);
- Data on education or skills attained by participants;

- Measures of improved health status;
- Estimates of the fiscal savings resulting from reduced fertility rate among at-risk teens;

Using these types of measures means that the data collection and processing procedures will have to be set up when the program is set up. That will require staff time—usually very scarce during the initial phases of a new program.

Educating the Public

Selling entrepreneurial policy solutions is not easy. The media concentrates on features of the economy that are visually memorable—the unemployment line or the factory closing—rather than on the causes of unemployment, and they have avoided topics that cannot be explained in a one minute news segment.[3]

Therefore, the problem, the stages of its solution and the concrete evidence of success should be publized relentlessly. Budget messages, special press conferences, state of the state messages, and other communications should all be structured around the same theme.

In 1983 Governor Robert Graham of Florida made education his top priority. He established a goal that Florida would reach the top quartile in education by 1986. The theme became: "Education Means Business." The year 1983 was declared the year of education. The budget document emphasized the theme; the state-of-the-state address emphasized it; and all major speeches of the governor supported it. But 1983 was not the only year that the governor stressed the point. He did so in 1981, 1982, and 1984. The message got across. In 1983 the legislature appropriated $250 million for education reform in Florida.

Part of plan to educate the public about an entrepreneurial development strategy must be to highlight the contributions made by local entrepreneurs to local development. This might take the form of governors' annual "entrepreneurial awards" honoring innovations and inventions, and the publicizing of employment creation and business formation data as well as traditional unemployment and business failure figures. These actions would counter the emphasis traditionally given to less effective symbols of economic activity. In the long run, education of the public must be accomplished through formal entrepreneurial education programs in high schools and colleges.

Influence Legislation

Legislation can be passed providing the public and legislators with better information about the consequences of a proposed initiative. For example:

- For several years, New York State had been considering cutting back or abolishing a huge tax-exemption program that gave large benefits to major corporations moving into the state and to corporations that were considering moving out. In effect, the program paid large businesses in New York State to publicly declare that they were considering moving out because New York was a bad place to do business in order to get the tax credit. And the program paid well too—nearly $50 million a year in tax expenditures. In 1981 Tiffany's—the Fifth Avenue jeweller—approached the Job Incentive Board, which managed the program, and argued that it would have to move some 200 "back-office" jobs out of Manhattan to Newark, New Jersey, unless it was given some subsidy to cover the cost of rehabilitating two floors of its building. It was granted a 10-year tax abatement worth more than 8 million dollars ($40,000 per job toward rehabilitation of one of the world's most valuable buildings!). It is, perhaps, not surprising that this received considerable media attention and within a year the program had been abolished.
- Louisiana had been considering legislation to relax banking regulations that forbade a bank from crossing parish boundaries. Legislation to allow multi-bank holding companies had been mired in committee for several years and was regarded by most legislators as a big bank/small bank issue that was best avoided. In 1984, as part of a major economic development initiative, the same legislation was offered. But this time, it was supported on the grounds that reform of the finance sector in that state was vital to its long-run growth prospects (Chapter 5). The legislation passed in 1984.
- Until 1984 postsecondary vocational education was funded in Florida the same way that it is funded in every other state— according to the fulltime equivalent number of students enrolled in the class. In 1984 Florida passed legislation that requires placement rates from every class to be measured. Funds will now be distributed according to how well the institution has placed students in jobs. In most states, institutions have successfully resisted performance measures. Florida was able to overcome this resistance by publicizing the wide disparities

in placement rates among institutions and by including the initiative as part of a well-organized education strategy.

Many issues have become log-jammed, and little progress seems possible. However, there are opportunities to redefine the debate in a way that allows resolution. For example, in many western states the issue of who gets water and who pays for it has preoccupied state and local governments for many years. The passage of time has only made the issue more acute. However, establishing a market for water rights to replace the state's allocative procedure can broaden the support for taking action.

Retain Existing Support

No economic development strategy will succeed if the existing businesses in the state view it as against their interests. For many established groups, an entrepreneurial policy sounds threatening. The greatest challenge in implementing this strategy is to maintain the support of traditional business and labor coalitions. There are two ways in which opposition can be tempered (other than including measures that directly help those harmed by the development process outlined in Chapter 6): 1) involve established leaders in the policy formulation process; and 2) include in the strategy elements that are likely to be of direct interest to economic interest groups.

Participation in the policy process. A danger inherent in involving business and labor groups in the policy process is that they will arrive at policies that protect themselves from further competition rather than policies that improve the entrepreneurial environment. This danger can be reduced if the policy agenda is carefully defined. For example, in 1983, when Arizona was developing an economic policy agenda that needed public support, it convened a policy forum of business and labor leaders and entrepreneurs. One of the task forces was to look specifically at the availability of venture capital for new enterprise. As a result of the meeting, administration of state regulations was changed to make new over-the-counter stock available, and entrepreneurs became part of the business community that was regularly consulted.

Including issues with broad support. Many issues are important to all aspects of the business community, both old and new. These include the quality of education, the condition of public works, and the control of health care. By involving the business community broadly in the formulation of these "motherhood" issues, support for the strategy can be broadened and the strength of the opposition blunted.

EPILOGUE

An entrepreneurial economy is not the natural condition. Karl Marx predicted that capitalists would bury competition. Joseph Schumpeter, the economist who introduced the entrepreneur into a theory of development and certainly not a Marxist, also believed that the links between government and special interest groups would proceed, inexorably, and replace entrepreneurship with an inflexible, corporate-socialist state. Economist Mancur Olson has found that the older a state, the more entrenched are the special interest groups, the less entrepreneurial is its environment, and the more slowly grows its income.[4]

Periods of rapid technological progress shake up the structure of special interests, weakening some established ones and sowing the seeds of new ones. The current technological revolution presents states with an opportunity to reestablish entrepreneurial economies to revive their faltering economies and to expand the opportunities for more of their citizens. The opportunity will not last forever. Change is a chance for economic revitalization, not a danger feared for its unfamiliarity.

However well designed is the state's development strategy, it guarantees neither prosperity nor job security for all the state's residents. But in the long-run, employment opportunities and wealth will be greater under an entrepreneurial strategy than under any alternative approach to development.

NOTES

1. The necessity of a trade-off between the two goals of improving equity and increasing efficiency is central to traditional equilibrium economics. In static equilibrium, one person can gain only if another loses. In the dynamic model described in the book, the trade-off is not inevitable. Because many of the barriers to entrepreneurship have been erected by interests powerful enough to use the political process, lowering those barriers will increase the dynamic efficiency of the economy and extend opportunities to the less powerful.

2. In fact, the recipient may not be particularly pleased because he or she is likely to have been charged a rate of interest above the average because of the higher risk. Since most businesspersons underestimate their own risk, they probably feel overcharged.

3. They contribute to economic misunderstanding by routinely reporting economic statistics without mentioning their limitations, distortions, and irrelevance. Because negative features make better stories than positive ones, we are exposed to more stories about the "dark side" of development than about its wealth enhancing aspects.

4. Olson 1982.

BIBLIOGRAPHY

Aronson, Richard J., *Public Finance* (New York: McGraw Hill, 1985)

Alchian, Armen, and Allen, William, *Exchange and Production: Competiton, Coordination, and Control: 2nd Edition* (Belmont: Wadwsorth Publishing Company, 1977)

Armington, Catherine, and Odle, Marjorie, "Sources of Job Growth: A New Look at the Small Business Role," (*Commentary*, National Council for Urban Economic Development, Fall,1982)

Armstrong, J.Scott, *Long Range Forecasting From Crystal Ball to Computer* (New York: Wiley Interscience, 1978)

Arrow, Kenneth, *The Limits of Organization* (New York: W.W. Norton and Co., 1974)

Babbitt, Bruce, "Grass Roots Industrial Policy" (*Issues in Science and Technology*, 1984)

Bahl, Roy, *Financing State and Local Government in the 1980's* (New York: Oxford University Press, 1984)

Barro, Robert, *Macroeconomics.* McGraw Hill, New York, 1985.

Bates, Timothy, M., *Black Capitalism: A Quantitative Analysis* (New York: Praeger, 1973)

Bates, Timothy, M. and Bradford, William, *Financing Black Economic Development* (New York: Academic Press, 1979)

Baumol, W.J. , "Entrepreneurship in Economic Theory" (*American Economic Review*, May 1969)

Bearse, Peter, "A New Paradigm for State Economic Development Policy" (*New England Journal of Business and Economics*, 2, 1976, pp. 37-57)

Bearse, Peter J., and Konopko, D., "A Comparative Analysis of State Programs to Promote New Technology Based Enterprise" (*New England Journal of Business and Econmics*, Spring, 1979)

Bell, Daniel and Kristol, Irving, eds., *The Crisis in Economic Theory* (New York: Harper and Row, 1981)

Berney, Robert E., *The Cost of Government Regulation on Small Business, An Update* (Working Paper 1180-1, Washington: Washington State University, 1980)

Birch, David L., *The Job Generation Process* (Cambridge: MIT Program on Neighborhood and Regional Change) 1978

Bluestone, Barry, *The Deindustrialization of America* (New York: Basic Books, 1982)

Bluestone, Barry and Harrison, Bennett, 1980, *Capital and Communities: The Causes and Consequences of Private Disinvestment* (Washington, D.C: Progressive Alliance Publications, April, 1980)

Boas Max, and Chain, Steve, *Big Mac: The Unauthorized Biography of McDonalds* (New York: Mentor Books, 1976)

Bosworth, B. and Duesenberry, J., *Capital Needs in the Seventies*, (Washington, D.C. : The Brookings Institute, 1975)

Botkin, James, Dimancescu, Dan, and Stata, Ray , *The Innovators: Rediscovering America's Creative Energy* (New York: Harper and Row, 1984)

Brealey, R. and Myers, S., *Principles of Corporate Finance* (McGraw Hill Book Company, New York, 1979)

Brown, Paul, B, "Entrepreneurship 101" (*Forbes*, September 24, 1984, pp. 174-8)

Business Week, "States Stop Playing Detective for Investors" (*Business Week*, July 16, 1984, p. 131-2)

Business Week, "The Drive to Deregulate Taxicabs" (*Business Week*, July 2, 1984, p.92-3)

Cagan, Phillip, "The Reduction in Inflation and the Magnitude of Unemployment," in Contemporary Economic Problems, edited by William Fellner (Washington D.C: American Enterprise Institute, 1977)

Calonious, Erik, L. , "Britain Moving to Reverse Its Drain of Scientific Talent" (*Wall Street Journal*, May 27, 1984)

Calvo, Guillermo A., and Wellisz, Stanislaw, Technology, Entrepreneurs, and Firm Size," (*Quarterly Journal of Economics*, December, 1980)

Carley, William, M. , "People Express Flies Into Airlines' Big Time in Just 3 Years Aloft," (*Wall Street Journal*, March 30, 1984, p.1)

Clarkson, Kenneth and Meiners, Roger E. , "Distortions in Official Unemployment Statistics: Implications for Public Policy Making" (Research Monograph No. 3, Texas A and M University Center for Education and Research on Free Enterprise, 1979)

Craig, Steven G. and Sailors, Joel, W. , "A Destructive War Between the States" (*Wall Street Journal*, January, 1985)

Curry, Timothy, "The Performance of Bank Holding Companies," in *The Bank Holding Company Movement to 1978: A Compendium*, Staff Study, Governors of the Federal Reserve System, 1978.

Curtis, Carol, "Power Play" (*Forbes*, Sept 10, 1984, p. 160)

Daniels, Belden, and Kieschnick, Michael, *Development Finance: A Primer for Policy Makers, Parts I,II, and III,* (Washington, D.C: National Rural Center, 1979)

Deeks, John, *The Small Firm Owner-Manager: Entrepreneurial Behavior and Management Practice* (New York: Praeger Publisher, 1976)

Diebold, John, *Making the Future Work* (New York: Simon and Schuster, 1984)

Downs, Anthony, *An Economic Theory of Democracy* (New York: Harper and Row, 1957)

Doyle, Dennis, and Finn, Chester , "American Schools and the Future of Local Control" (*The Public Interest,* Fall 1984, pp.77-95)

Drucker, Peter, *Management* (London, Pan Books, 1979)

Drucker, Peter, *Toward the Next Economics and Other Essays* (New York: Harper and Row, 1981)

Drucker, Peter, "Europe's High Tech Delusion" (*Wall Street Journal* Sept 14, 1984)

Eastburn, David P., and John J. Balles, "Survey III: Commercial Bank," in Financing Small Business, Federal Reserve System, 1958.

Economist, "Blessed are the Entrepreneurs" (*Economist,* Dec.22, 1984, pp.100-01)

Economist, "Fast Fries or High Tech?" (*Economist,* June 16, 1984, p.12)

Economist, "Towards Fuller Employment" (*Economist,* July 28, 1984, pp. 19-22)

Economist, "Peasants Rising" (*Economist,* Feb.2, 1985)

Ehrenberg, R.G. and Oaxaca, R.L., "Unemployment Insurance, Duration of Unemployment, and Subsequent Wage Gain" (*American Economic Review,* December 1976, pp. 754-66)

Ellwood, David, T and Summers, Laurence A., "Poverty in America: Is Welfare the Answer to the Problem?" (Paper delivered to the Conference on Poverty and Policy: Retrospect and Prospects, held in Willimsburg Virginia, Dec. 6-8, 1984)

Farrell, Kevin, "There's No Stopping Now" (*Venture,* February, 1985, pp. 40-8)

Felsenfeld, Carl, *Banking Business and Barbicans,* Citibank, New York, 1980.

Flaim, Paul O., "The Effect of Demographic Changes on the Nation's Unemployment" (*Monthly Labor Review,* March 1979, pp.13-23)

Flender, John and Morse, Richard , *The Role of New Technical Enterprises in the U.S. Economy* (Cambridge: MIT, 1978)

Freeman, Christopher, "The Role of Small Business in Innovation in the United Kingdom Since 1945," Committee of inquiry on Small Firms, Research Report No. 6, London 1971.

Fortune, editors, *Working Smarter* (New York: Penguin Books, 1982)

Friedman, Robert, and Schweke, William, eds, *Expanding the Opportunity to Produce* (Washington D.C: Corporation for Enterprise Development, 1981)

Friedman, Milton, and Friedman, Rose, *Tyrany of the Status Quo* (New York: Harcourt, Brace Jovanovich, 1984)

Fuerbringer, Jonathan, "How to Read the Economy" (*New York Times*, Nov 8, 1981)

Garn, Harvey A., *The Renaissance of Concern for Small Business Enterprise in the United States* (Washington D.C: Working Paper 1355-1 The Urban Institute, Fedruary, 1980)

Garn, Harvey A, and Ledebur, Larry, *The Small Business Sector in Economic Development* (Washington, D.C: The Urban Institute, 1980)

Gellman Research Associates, Inc., *Indicators of International Trends in Technological Innovation* (Washington, D.C: 1976)

Gilder, George, "Fear of Capitalism" (*Inc*, Sept, 1984, pp.87-94)

Gilder, George, *Spirit of Enterprise* (New York: Basic Books, 1984)

Goodman, Robert, *The Last Entrepreneurs* (Boston: The South End Press, 1979)

Gordon, David, *The Working Poor* (Washington, D.C: Council of State Planning Agencies, 1979)

Greenfield, Sidney M., and Strickon, A. , "A New Paradigm for the Study of Entrepreneurship and Social Change" (*Economic Development and Social Change*, 1981)

Grossman, Ilene K. , *Initiatives in State Economic Development* (Chicago: Council of State Governments, 1984)

Gupta, Udayan, "Redefining the Intrapreneur" (*Venture*, March, 1985, pp. 45-8)

Guttentag, Jack M., and Edward S. Herman, "Bank Structure and Performance," *The Bulletin*, Institute of Finance, Graduate School of Public Administration, New York University, February 1967.

Hansen, Derek, *Banking and Small Business Finance*, (Washington, D.C: Council of State Planning Agencies, 1981)

Harrison, Bennett and Kantor, S., "The Political Economy of State Job-Creation Business Incentives," (*Journal of the American Institute of Planners*, October, 1978)

Hayek, Friedrich, A., "The Uses of Knowledge In Society" in *Individualism and the Economic Order* (Chicago: University of Chicago Press, 1948)

Hayek, Friedrich, A., "The Moral Element in Free Enterprise" (Paper presented in the 66th National Congress of American Industry, Dec 6, 1961)

Heggerstad, A., and Steven Rhoads, "Multi-Market Interdependence and Local Market Competition in Banking," *Review of Economics and Statistics*, Vol. LX November 1978.

Heyne, Paul, *The Economic Way of Thinking* (Chicago: Science Research Associates, Inc. 1980)

U.S. Congress Joint Economic Committee, "Location of High Technology Firms and Regional Economic Development" (Washington, D.C: U.S. Government Printing Office, 1982)

Jencks, Christopher, "The Hidden Prosperity of the 1970's" (*Public Interest*, Fall 1984, pp. 37-61)

Johnson, Chalmers, ed, *The Industrial Policy Debate* (San Francisco: Institute for Contemporary Policy, 1984)

Kendrick, John, "Productivity Gains Will Continue" (*Wall Street Journal*, August 29, 1984)

Kent, Calvin, ed., *The Environment for Entrepreneurship* (Lexington: Lexington Books, 1984)

Kieschnick, Michael, *Taxes and Growth* (Council of State Planning Agencies, Washington, D.C., 1981)

Kieschnick, Michael, *Venture Capital* (Washington, D.C.: Council of State Planning Agencies, 1980)

Kilby, Peter, *Entrepreneurship and Economic Development,* (New York: Free Press, 1971)

Kirzener, Isreal, M. , *Competition and Entrepreneurship* (Chicago, University of Chicago Press)

Kirzener, I.M., *Competition and Entrepreneurship* (Chicago: University of Chicago Press, 1973)

Kirzener, Isreal, M. , *The Economic Point of View* (Kansas City: Sheed and Ward, Inc.)

Kirzener, Isreal M., "The Entrepreneurial Process" (in Calvin Kent ed. *The Environment for Entrepreneurship* Lexington: Lexington Books, 1984)

Klein, Burton, *Dynamic Economics* (Cambridge: Harvard University Press, 1977)

Kosters, Marvin H., "Government Regulations: Present State and Need for Industrial Reform." in Wachter, Michael L., and Wachter, Susan M., eds.

135

Toward a New U.S Industrial Policy (Philadelphia: University of Pennsylvania Press, 1983)

Lachmann, Ludwig, M., *Capital Expectations, and the Market Process* (Kansas City: Sheed Andrews and McMeel, Inc. 1977)

Lauch, Louis H., and Neil B. Murphy, "A Test of the Impact of Branching on Deposit Variability," *Journal of Finance and Quantitative Analysis*, Vol. 5 September, 1970.

Leff, Nathaniel, H., "Entrepreneurship and Economic Development: The Problem Revisited" (*Journal of Economic Literature*, March 1979, pp. 46-64)

Levine, Sumner, N., *The Dow Jones-Irwin Business and Investment Almanac, 1983* (Homewood: Dow Jones Irwin, 1983)

Littlechild, Stephen, *The Fallacy of the Mixed Economy: An "Austrian" Critiquie of Conventional Economics and Government Policy* (San Francisco: Cato Institute, 1979)

Litvak, Lawrence and Daniels, Belden, *Innovations in Development Finance*, (Washington D.C: Council of State Planning Agencies, 1980)

Magaziner, Ira, and Robert Reich, *Minding America's Business*, Basic Books, New York, 1982.

Mansfield, et. al., *Technology Transfer, Productivity and Economic Policy* (New York, W.W. Norton and Co. 1982)

Mckenzie, Richard, and Tullock, Gordon , *Modern Political Economy* (McGraw Hill Book Company, New York, 1978)

McKenzie, Richard, *Fugitive Industry: The Economics and Politics of Deindustrialization* (Cambridge, Ballinger Publishing Co., 1984)

Minsky, Tom, "The Entrepreneur: Scooping Up Cold Cash," (*Esquire*, March, 1985, p. 58)

Morris, R., and D.C. Mueller, "The Corporation, Competition, and the Invisible Hand," *Journal of Economic Literature*, Vol. 18, No. 1, March 1980.

Navarro, Peter, *The Policy Game* (New York, Wiley, 1984)

National Federation of Independent Businesses, *Report on Small Businesses in American Cities*, (NFIB, 1981)

O'Neill, Hugh, *Creating Opportunity: Reducing Dependency through Economic Development* (Washington D.C: Council of State Planning Agencies, 1985)

Olson, Mancur, *The Rise and Decline of Nations* (New Haven: Yale University Press, 1982)

Patricoff, Alan J., "The Role of Venture Capital" (*Institutional Investor*, December, 1979)

Peirce, Neal R and Hagstrom, Jerry, *The Book of America* (New York: W.W. Norton and Co., 1983)

Peters, Thomas J., and Robert H. Waterman, *In Search of Excellence*, New York, Harper and Row, 1982.

Posner, Richard, *Antitrust Law* (Chicago: University of Chicago Press)

Quinn, James B., "Technological Innovation, Entrepreneurship, and Strategy" (*Sloan Management Review*, Spring, 1979)

Radford, R.A. , "The Economic Organization of a POW Camp" (*Economica*, November, 1945, pp. 189-201)

"Home Grown Protectionism Exposed." (*Reason*, January 1985, p. 12)

Riche, Richard, W., Hecker, Daniel E, and Burgan, John U. , "High Technology Today and Tomorrow: A Small Slice of the Employment Pie" (*Monthly Labor Review*, November 1983, pp. 50-8)

Richman, Tom, "What America Needs is a Few Good Business Failures" (*Inc*, September, 1983, pp.63-72)

Rohatyn, Felix, *The Twenty Year Century*, Basic Books, New York, 1984.

Rozen, Miriam, "A Second Way to the Top" (*New York Times*, February 10, 1985, p. F21)

Rukeyser, Louis, *What's Ahead for the American Economy* (Simon and Schuster, New York, 1983)

Russell, Sabin, "Now Its the World's Turn" (*Venture*, September, 1984, pp. 46-61)

Rydenfelt, Sven, "Today Sweden Looks to the Entrepreneurs," (*Wall Street Journal*, Dec. 5, 1984, p.31)

Savas, E.S, *Privatizing the Public Sector* (Chatham, Chatham House Publishing, 1982)

Small Business Adminstration, *Small Business and Innovation* (Washington D.C: Office of the Chief Counsel for Advocacy, Small Business Administration, 1979)

Schelling, Thomas, *Micromotives and Macrobehavior* (New York: W.W. Norton Inc., 1978)

Scherer, F.M., *Industrial Market Structure and Economic Performance* (Chicago: Rand McNally, 1980)

Schmenner, Roger, *The Manufacturing Location Decision: Evidence from Cincinnati and New England* (Washington D.C: U.S. Economic Development Administration, March 1978)

Schultz, Theodore, *Investing in People* (Berkeley: University of California Press, 1982)

Schumpeter, Joseph, *Capitalism, Socialism, and Democracy* (Harper and Row, New York, 1942)

Sekera, June, *Corporate Initiatives in New Business Development: Five Case Studies* (Corporation for Enterprise Development, April, 1981)

Serrin, William, "Jobs Increase in Number, but Trends are Said to be Leaving Many Behind" (*New York Times*, October 15, 1984, p.18)

Shand, Alexander, *The Capitalist Alternative: An Intorduction to Neo-Austrian Economics* (New York: New York University Press, 1984)

Shapero, Albert, "Numbers that Lie" (*Inc*, May 1981, p. 16-7)

Shapero, Albert, "Entrepreneurship" in *Proceedings of the Community Economic Development Strategies Conference,* 1983 (Iowa: North Central Regional Center for Rural Development, Iowa State University, 1983)

Shapero, Albert, "The Entrepreneurial Event," in Calvin Kent, ed. *The Environment for Entrepreneurship* (Lexington: Lexington Books, 1984)

Shapero, Albert and Gigierano, Joseph, *Exits and Entries: A Study in Yellow Pages Journalism* (College of Adminstrative Sciences, Ohio State University, July, 1982)

Shaw, Jane, "The Deepening Mystery of the Savings Rate" (*Business Week,* August 6, 1984, p.68)

Shull, Bernard, "Changes in Commercial Banking Structure and Small Business Lending," *Interagency Task Force on Small Business Finance,* Washington D.C., 1982.

Smith, Adam, *The Wealth of Nations* (New York: Penguin Classics, 1974)

Smith, Rodney, *Troubled Waters: Financing Water in the West* (Washington D.C: Council of State Planning Agencies, 1985)

Sobieski, John Daniel, "Cab Scam" (*Reason,* March, 1985, pp. 37-41)

Solomon, Ezra, *Beyond the Turning Point: The U.S. Economy in the 1980's* (San Francisco: W.H. Freeman and Co.)

Solomon, Ezra, and Pringle, John H., *An Introduction to Financial Management* (Santa Monica: Goodyear Publishing Co., 1979)

Sowell, Thomas, *Knowledge and Decisions* (New York: Basic Books, 1980)

Sowell, Thomas, *Markets and Minorities* (New York: Basic Books, 1981)

Sowell, Thomas, *Pink and Brown People* (Stanford: Hoover Institution Press, 1981)

Spadaro, Louis M. , *New Directions in Austrian Economics* (Kansas City: Sheed, Andrews, and McMeel, Inc.)

Stigler, George J. , *The Citizen and the State: Essays on Regulation* (Chicago: University of Chicago Press, 1975)

Stigler, George J., "The Theory of Economic Regulations" (*Bell Journal of Economics and Management Science,* Spring 1971)

Stoll, Hans, and Walter, James, *Tax Incentives for Small Business* (Philadelphia: University of Pennsylvania, 1980)

Straszheim, Mahlon, "The Cost of Capital and the Market Power of Firms" (*Review of Economics and Statistics,* 1978, pp. 209-17)

Taggart, Robert, *A Fisherman's Guide: An Assessment of Training and Remediation Strategies* (Kalamazoo: W.E. Upjohn Institute for Employment Research, 1981)

Index

Corporation, and innovation from retained earnings, 70
Cotton, vii
Craig, Steven, 56
Crime rate, as economic indicator, 33
Cultural services, as nontraded valuable good, 39
Curriculum approval, 96

Data collection and processing, part of initial program, 125
Day care, identification of regulatory barriers to, 60
Debt capital, 75–78
Debt financing, for public works, 110
Debt service, 37, 111
Decisionmaking, and responsibility, 103–05
Dedicated revenues, 111
Demand assessment, 106
Dependency reduction strategy, 124–25
Depreciation allowances, 68
Deregulation, 60
Development finance programs, 67
Development policies, and defining problems, 120–22; and dislocations, 120; and job creation, 34–37; jurisdictional issues in, 17; more than job growth, 12; opponents of, 3; politics of, 2; public role in, 24; traditional 1
Development programs, evaluation criteria for, 47; and growth industries, 38–42; targeted to growth industries, 27
Development strategies, 4, 46, 59–61, 120–28
Displaced workers, 2, 21, 28, 96–98
Distributional consequences of entrepreneurial activity, 21–22
Diversification of economy, 59
Dividend income, 68, 69
Drop out rates, 91, 124
Drucker, Peter, 85

Durable goods manufacturing sector, see Manufacturing

Earmarked revenues, for infrastructure investments, 113
Earnings of graduates, 90
Eastern Airlines, 19
Economic capacity, measurement of, 29
Economic development, definition of, 3, 12; displacement caused by, 16; and education policy, viii, 119, see also Education; and entrepreneurship, 34; and expanding economic opportunities, 16, 55; goal of, 1; and job creation, 27; process of, 13–16; and state strategies, viii; traditional views of, 27–50
Economic displacement by innovation, 19
Economic expansion, in Mississippi, vii-viii
Economic performance, indicators of, 27, 33, 45
Economic regulations, review and reform of, 59; see also Banks, regulation of; Regulations
Economic stabilization, 28
Economically disadvantaged, 89, 120; see also Low-income people
Economy, diagnoses of, 27–34
Education, 46; and entrepreneurial development, 1; expenditures as part of development budgets, 27, 91; in Florida a priority, 125; funding of, 90, 96; investments in, 1, 87–88; of population, 39; quality of, 127; role of public sector in, 5, see also Education and training; as state activity, 5, 86, 104, 124; Workforce attainment of, 33
Education and skills, 85–87, 124
Education and training, central part of state development policy, viii, 95–98; with government as information provider, 88–89; gov-